101 things to buy before you die

101 things to buy before you die

CHARLOTTE WILLIAMSON
AND MAGGIE DAVIS

NEW
HOLLAND

This edition first published in 2009 by New Holland Publishers (UK) Ltd
London • Cape Town • Sydney • Auckland
www.newhollandpublishers.com

Garfield House, 86–88 Edgware Road, London, W2 2EA, United Kingdom
80 McKenzie Street, Cape Town, 8001, South Africa
Unit 1, 66 Gibbes Street, Chatswood, NSW 2067, Australia
218 Lake Road, Northcote, Auckland, New Zealand

A catalogue record for this book is available from the British Library

ISBN 978 1 84773 512 6

Although the publishers have made every effort to ensure that information contained in this book was meticulously
researched and correct at the time of going to press, they accept no responsibility for any inaccuracies, loss, injury
or inconvenience sustained by any person using this book as reference.

Publishing Director: Rosemary Wilkinson
Publisher: Aruna Vasudevan
Project Editor: Julia Shone
Editor: Cosima Hibbert
Cover design: Nick Castle Design
Designers: Gülen Shevki-Taylor, Sue Rose, Sarah Williams
Production: Sarah Kulasek, Melanie Dowland
DTP: Tammy Warren

Reproduction by Modern Age Repro House, Hong Kong
Printed and bound in Thailand by Kyodo Nation Printing Services Co. Ltd

10 9 8 7 6 5 4 3 2 1

Picture credits

With special thanks to Esther Adams, Olivia Bergin, Ruth Caven and Alfred Tong.

All images of products kindly supplied by the respective companies, except for those images credited below. Additional credits for
photographers and companies are also given: t=top, b=bottom, l=left, r=right, c=centre

Front cover: Christian Louboutin stiletto; Lipstick Queen, photo copyright © Poppy King; Diamond Ring, Wint & Kidd; Hermès Birkin handbag; Pol Roger Cuvée
champagne; Scooter, photo courtesy of Piaggio. Back cover: Bocca Marylin Lips sofa, photo courtesy of Edra; Cartier Tankissme watch; Aston Martin DB5.

Rob Greig: 2, 3, 10, 16(b), 34(t), 35(b), 36, 45, 53, 58, 63(t), 63(c), 63(b), 64(b), 67, 68(t), 68(b), 69(t), 69(bl), 69(br), 70(t), 70(b), 71(t), 71(c), 72(t), 76, 81(t), 98, 106,
125, 126, 127, 128, 136(t), 136(b), 137, 144, 149(t), 149(b), 153

Scooter, photo courtesy of Piaggio: 1, 157; Tom Dixon Ball Chandelier for Swarovski, photographed by Andrea Ferrari: 6; Goyard hand-painted monogram copyright © Goyard: 9; Lanvin dress, photo copyright © Christopher Moore Ltd: 11, 28; Kilgour suit, photo copyright © Sean Ellis: 13; Schiesser boxer shorts, photo
by Peartree Digital Ltd: 16; Cadolle Bra, photo copyright © Louisa Parry: 17; MaxMara catwalk image, © Christopher Moore Ltd: 22; Earnest Sewn Jeans / Xavier
Brunet: 25; Chanel catwalk image, © Christopher Moore Ltd: 29; Burberry Raincoat, photo copyright © Mario Testino: 31; Charvet Shirts, photo rights reserved
(AMC): 32; Almas Caviar, photo courtesy of Cavier House & Prunier: 41, 42; Kopi Luwak Coffee, photo copyright © 1005 Todd Dalton & Edible Ltd: 49; Gelato
© Envision/Corbis: 50; Spice © Peter Adams/Zefa/Corbis: 54; Tea, photo copyright © John Rice Photography, www.johnricephoto.com: 55; Lipstick Queen,
photo copyright © Poppy King; Ruby & Millie Cheek Color, photo by Peartree Digital Ltd: 61; Chanel Powder Blush, photo by Peartree Digital Ltd: 61; M.A.C lip-
stick, photo by Peartree Digital Ltd: 75; Barcelona chair, photocourtesy of The Aram Store: 84; Arne Jacobsen 3107 chair, photo courtesy of
Twentytwentyone.com: 85 (tl); Lounge Chair and Ottoman, design Charles and Ray Eames, 1956, photo: Hans Hanse: 85 (b); Coffee Tables, photos courtesy of
Aram: 88(t), 88(b); Global Knife Block, photo courtesy of John Lewis: 95; Amish Quilt, photo copyright © Lonely Planet Images / Richard l'Anson: 101;Le
Corbusier Sofa, photo courtesy of Twentytwentyone.com: 104(t); Jasper Morrison Cappelini Elan sofa, photo courtesy of SCP Ltd: 104 (b); Bocca Marylin Lips
sofa, photo courtesy of Edra: 105; Tablecloths, photo courtesy of Busatti: 107; Portuguese Tiles, photo courtesy of www.portugal2u.com (Oscar Amara): 109;
Legendary Lesotho Diamond, photo courtesy of Harry Winston / © Hans Gissinger 2004: 116; Gems © Royalty-free/Corbis: 117; Gem Palace showroom, cour-
tesy of the Gem Palace: 117; Mikimoto Pearls, photo courtesy of Mikimoto: 120; Breitling Bentley 6.75, photo courtesy of Watches of Switzerland: 123; Louis
Vuitton Luggage, photo copyright © Antoine Jarrier: 138 (t); Comme des Garçons wallets, photo courtesy of Purple PR: 150; Aston Martin, photo courtesy of
Aston Martin; 151, 155; Apache Skis, photo courtesy of Snow and Rock (0845 1000 1000, www.snowandrock.com): 158; Tennis racquet courtesy of Babolat
Vs: 159; Florence Broadhurst wallpaper, photo courtesy of Florence Broadhurst: 160.

Contents

Introduction

Welcome to the third edition of *101 Things to Buy Before You Die*. Much has changed in the world of consumerism since we first published in 2006. Fast fashion, for one thing – most of us have far too much stuff, and over-flowing wardrobes suddenly feel so un-chic. Ethical concerns have also crept into our consumer consciousness. But, most importantly, the global recession has drastically changed our shopping habits, quite possibly forever. For a start, we all have less money in our pockets – or at least feel like we do – and this is impacting our choices. Gone are the days of disposable trends, replaced by a savvier attitude to spending.

Consuming less – and, ergo, the best – has always been our guiding principle. Buying half a dozen cheap frocks at £30 a pop is a false economy: they might look – and indeed feel – great on the first wearing, but what of the fifth, the sixth? Heck, will they even make it that long? On the other hand, the right designer LBD will last for years, decades, even generations; the same can be said for more practical products such as the right toaster or sofa – just as disposable as those cheap frocks, but need this be the case?

In our updated edition, we have made a conscious decision to include more affordable items. A £2.99 mascara, for instance; a super-dooper £29 moisturiser; five-star-hotel-quality bed linen (but for a fraction of the price) from Marks & Spencer. We have also included more ethical and ecologically aware products: gold and even nail polish are new entries this time round.

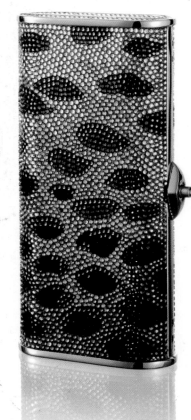

We can't pretend that much in this book doesn't cost a lot. But – and this is a huge but – we strongly believe these items are an investment. A Hermès bag, for instance, will last a lifetime. As will a Duxiana bed, or a bespoke suit from Henry Poole. There are also a few new categories: coats, white shirts, blusher, bath oil. We've kept some of our frivolous favourites: the £4,000 Goyard trunk, which remains utterly gorgeous. But a girl can dream!

For both of us, shopping is an unashamed passion. As lifestyle journalists, we're forever being asked to track down the top products available on the market. We obsessively jot down tidbits of shopping information every time we hear them, whether it's the best paint colour for a front door, wrinkle-reducers that actually work, or chocolate that's good enough to make your toes curl with happiness. Think of us as slightly younger, less manic, and hopefully less ruthless, versions of Eddy and Patsy in *Ab Fab* when they went ballistic upon discovering the ultimate door handle in New York. We've gone bananas over *much* more ordinary things … such as the perfect mattress for a good night's sleep. Come to think of it, in such wearisome times, the perfect mattress is pretty crucial.

Hence this book. *101 Things to Buy Before You Die* is a collection of the very best in food, fashion, furniture and fun. Up to a point, our guide is subjective. We had one important rule: a bona fide justification for each of our choices. So we've asked specialist buyers and those in the know for their suggestions: some are spectacular and, of course, super-expensive; others

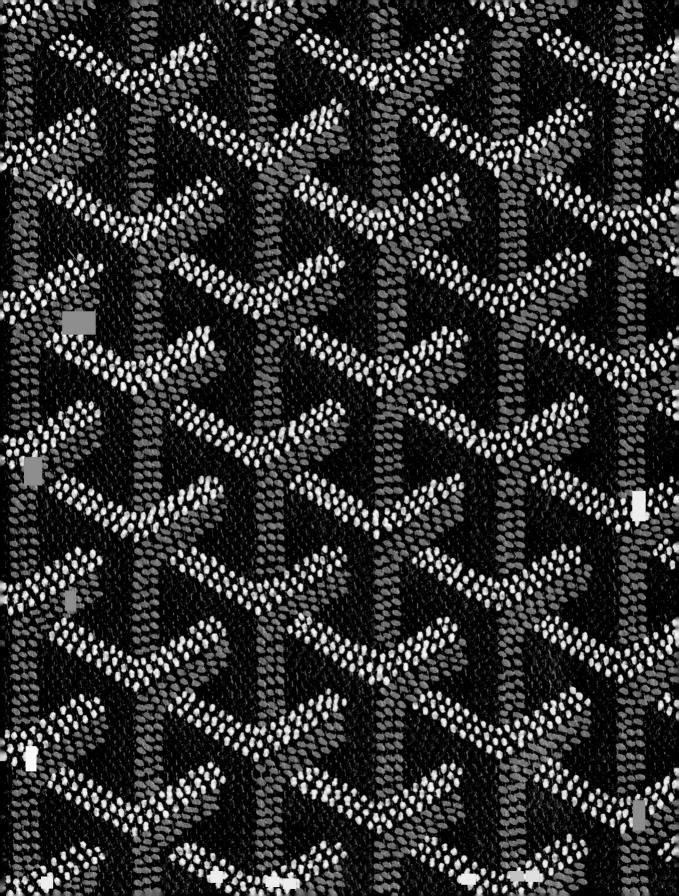

'*The more alternatives, the more difficult the choice.*'
Abbé d'Allainval,
French dramatist, 1700–53

surprisingly reasonable – proof that money doesn't always buy the best. Many of the items have been selected because of their cult status; others are more about heritage or craftsmanship. Each product includes a gorgeous illustration to inspire, plus two alternatives that are often more affordable. More importantly, each choice is unbiased – no company has paid to be in this guide.

Between us we've done a *lot* of shopping and much of it has been done abroad. As the Victorians demonstrated so gloriously on their Grand Tours of Europe, when they picked up bespoke marbled stationery in Florence and heavenly fragrances in Paris, a canny shopper knows that to get the best deals you need to go global. But if you don't have the time, or inclination, to source your spices in Jodphur (in India), that's where the internet comes in: global shopping at the click of a button.

The book is divided into seven sections for easy reference: Clothes, Food & drink, Beauty, Home, Jewellery, Shoes & accessories, and Leisure. The prices are in UK sterling, US dollars and euros, and in most cases they are rounded off to the nearest figure. To help further, we have included invaluable advice on shopping for certain purchases – what to look for when buying a diamond, for instance, or how a good glass of champagne should taste – plus tips on haggling and etiquette in a souk.

Everyone shops. Not everyone *likes* to shop, but they need to. Yet if done properly, shopping can be fun; even a stick-in-the-mud retrograde man would enjoy bartering in a bazaar or browsing calfskin luggage at Hermès in Paris. If you know what you're looking for – and where to look – shopping becomes hassle-free.

You may not agree with our choices, but hopefully you'll agree with our reasoning and start buying better stuff. If nothing else, *101 Things to Buy Before You Die* will make you a more discerning shopper.

Maggie Davis and Charlotte Williamson,
London, 2009

Clothes

*'The finest clothing made is a
person's skin but, of course, society
demands something more than this.'*

*Mark Twain, American author,
1835–1910*

Bespoke suit

Henry Poole

Where?

15 Savile Row, London, W1 • 00 44 207 734 5985 • www.henrypoole.com

How much?

From approx £2,915/$4,400/€3,315

There's no more grown-up, pivotal purchase a man can make than a handmade bespoke suit. The ultimate expression of power, professionalism and gentlemanliness, it is to men what the perfect little black dress is to women – a wardrobe staple that is timeless, effortless and easy. From the streets of Milan to Paris and London, Europe has a rich heritage of bespoke tailoring, but nowhere has quite the same reputation as London's Savile Row, the established home of the bespoke suit. But where do you go for the ultimate? It's tough to pinpoint the absolute best – there are now around 10 genuine bespoke tailors on Savile Row – but Henry Poole is certainly one of the most respected.

Henry Poole

The company, which celebrated its 200th anniversary in 2006, has been making bespoke suits for royalty ever since Edward VII (a renowned arbiter of taste) granted the company a royal warrant in the early 20th century. The process is thorough and meticulous: it takes at least three appointments to get the ideal suit. The tailor starts by taking your measurements to make a pattern for the body. This is finely tuned at the second fitting, where the tailor checks details, such as the distance between the back collar and the shoulders as well as the trouser break on the shoes. At the third fitting, final details and adjustments are made. The end result is a slick suit that fits like a second skin. As Henry Poole's Managing Director Simon Cundey says: 'The aim is to feel like you're not wearing a suit at all.'

Henry Poole showroom

KILGOUR

Kilgour

Where? 8 Savile Row, London, W1 • 00 44 207 734 6905 • www.kilgour.eu
How much? From approx £3,500/$5,300/€3,900

Founded in 1882, Kilgour, a brand that has dressed the likes of Fred Astaire, Cary Grant and, more recently, Hugh Grant and Bryan Ferry, has glided stylishly into the 21st century. In 2004, this Savile Row shop was refurbished, becoming a modern, minimalist space in which the suits hang like *objets d'art*, but the traditional tailoring methods remain the same. Every element of a Kilgour suit is bespoke, from cutting the cloth to the fine art of finishing. It is one of the last establishments on Savile Row that preserves the one tailor, one garment system, and it takes one of the 50 employed tailors at least 80 hours to complete a single suit.

HUNTSMAN

Where? 11 Savile Row, London, W1 • 00 44 207 734 7441
• www.h-huntsman.com
How much? From approx £3,895/$5,900/€4,420

Henry Huntsman established his business in 1849, specializing in breeches. The company was one of the first to receive a royal warrant, which was bestowed upon them in 1865 by the Prince of Wales. Huntsman's bespoke suits manage to stay abreast of current fashion trends, while maintaining a heritage of fine craftsmanship.

'**B**espoke v. *Past tense and a past participle of bespeak.* adj. *1. Custom-made. Said especially of clothes. 2. Making or selling custom-made clothes: a bespoke tailor.*'

Bespoke on a budget

Traditional British brand Gieves & Hawkes (1 Savile Row, W1; 00 44 207 434 2001; www.gievesandhawkes.com) provides a personal tailoring service that combines its ready-to-wear skills with your own requirements. At £695/$1,385/€1,117 for a two-piece suit, it is around a quarter of the price of a bespoke suit. Irish tailor Jonathan Quearney (7 Windmill Street, London W1; 00 44 207 631 5132; www.jonathanquearney.com) is also a master at whipping up a fine suit on a budget, and will make one to measure for well under £1000/$1,993/€1,464. If it's classic Savile Row style you require – but don't have the funds – head to David Saxby at vintage suit emporium Old Hat (66 Fulham Road, SW6; 00 44 207 610 6558), who will kit you out in the finest second-hand suit he can lay his hands on. Another option is to simply go ready-to-wear – our favourites currently include the razor-sharp styling of Etro, Prada and Jil Sander.

ORIGINS OF SAVILE ROW

Mayfair's long association with tailoring goes back to the late 1500s, when Robert Baker set up the street's first tailoring business and named Piccadilly after the pickadil, an Elizabethan shirt collar. Savile Row grew out of Lord Burlington's kitchen garden in 1695 and was named after his wife, Dorothy Savile, but its first tenants were military officers and physicians. It wasn't until 1733, that the first evidence of bespoke tailoring was recorded in the *Daily Post* and credited to Beau Brummel, now known as patron saint of the bespoke suit. From then on, tailors began to flourish along the street which, due to high rent and new businesses, has diminished somewhat to around 10 authentic bespoke tailors today.

Bikini

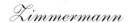

Where?

Select department stores worldwide •
www.net-a-porter.com • zimmermannwear.com

How much?

From £108/$154/€117

It may be just two minuscule pieces of Lycra but, fashion-wise, nothing causes quite as much pleasure and pain as buying a bikini. And while colour, print and shape are all important, the key thing to get right is fit.

High-profile Australian swimwear label Zimmermann is known for its bold, sexy styles and striking silhouettes. Set up by Sydney-based sisters Nicky and Simone Zimmermann in 1991, it is now the world's premier bikini brand thanks to its flattering cuts and quality fabrics.

MALIA MILLS

Where? 1031 Lexington Avenue, between 73rd and 74th Streets, New York, NY 10021 • 00 1 212 517 7485 • www.maliamills.com

How much? From £60/$115/€87

New York designer Malia Mills' bikini tops work just like a bra, each one featuring contouring seams for shape and a perfect fit; three sets of hook fastenings at the back and three different size straps, ranging from thin for small tops to thicker ones on D-cup pluses. Then there's the all-important addition of sliders, so you can adjust the strap length on your bikini top for the right amount of support. The bottoms also come in a range of shapes, fits and styles, so you can ensure you find the perfect pair to suit your shape.

'Everyone needs to go in with the attitude that you never know what will look good,' says Mills. 'You have to try on a little of everything, because you never know what might be the surprise hit. The same goes for colour: while you might think that a really pale girl will look best in a dark brown, she might be the perfect ice princess in a pale lilac, especially if that suits her personality.'

Zimmermann

ERES

Where? 2 Rue Tronchet, 75008, Paris, France • 00 33 1 47 42 28 82 • www.eresparis.com • Stores in USA, Japan and France

How much? From approx £170/$240/€180

These bikinis are subtle, streamlined and constructed from a unique body-contouring stretch fabric in a range of colours with simple shapes and an excellent fit.

' You know a bikini fits just right when you feel great: you want the bottom to be nice and smooth – if the fabric is wrinkling or bunching in the back, it's too big. You should be able to really move around in your top. Lift your arms up, and make sure you don't come out of the bottom. Bend over like you're picking up a towel and make sure you don't fall out. The one thing that you want to avoid is sacrificing fit for fashion.'

Malia Mills gives her expert advice on how to find the perfect bikini

Eres

A SHORT BIOGRAPHY OF THE BIKINI

Ever since the two-piece swimsuit, named after an A–bomb testing site called Bikini Atoll, was pioneered by engineer Louis Reard and fashion designer Jacques Heim in Paris in the mid-1940s, it has been one of the most important garments a woman needs to get right. Brigitte Bardot propelled it into the public eye when she was snapped frolicking around in a cream sculpted bikini in the 1956 film …*And God Created Woman*; Ursula Andress furthered its profile a few years later as the voluptuous bikini-clad Honey Ryder in *Dr No* (1962). In the 1970s, Norma Kamali injected disco glamour and introduced the thong bottom, which became an instant hit on the beaches of Rio. The 1980s saw power swimwear as worn by the athletically-built model Cindy Crawford, while a decade later, the pared-down simplicity of a neutral-toned Calvin Klein bikini was the ultimate in chic. But where does that leave us now? Luckily, with more choice, fabrics and designs than ever before. Today we have extensive, attractive bikini ranges in a multitude of shapes from the string to the classic triangle, available everywhere from high-street chains such as H&M, Gap and Topshop, to high-end designers like Pucci, Missoni and Dolce & Gabbana.

Boxer shorts

Schiesser

Where?
Bread & Honey, 205 Whitecross street, London EC1Y 8QP • 00 44 20 7253 4455 • Opening Ceremony, Opening Ceremony New York, 35 Howard Street, New York, NY10013 • 001 212 219 2688 • www.schiesser.com

How much?
Approx £29/$41.14/€31.18

Schiesser
boxer shorts

Specializing in fine-gauge cotton jersey underwear, German-brand Schiesser provides the most stylish boxer shorts around. Apart from the fine quality and easy shapes, what gives Schiesser its style credibility is the simple, graphic, retro packaging and its exclusivity – they are only available at a handful of small boutiques in London and New York. Who ever thought boxer shorts could be so desirable?

ZIMMERLI ROYAL CLASSIC
Where? www.zimmerli.com
How much? £35/$74/€36.95
This Swiss luxury underwear brand favoured by Prince Charles, Tom Cruise and Karl Lagerfeld has been at the forefront of developing mercerized cotton (a process whereby cotton thread is covered in polyester and treated in sodium hydroxide for extra lustre and strength). Its 'Royal Classic' boxers are the ultimate in style and comfort.

HANRO
Where? www.hanro.com
How much? £30/$62/€34
These luxurious Swiss-made mercerized cotton boxer shorts in a classic, very simple style are comfortable and cool, featuring an all-important supportive front and soft, elasticated waistband. Sleek and stylish.

And for the best swim trunks...
Where? www.vilebrequin.com
How much? £80/$120/€90
While women have a thousand and one bikini brands to choose from (see pages 14–15), men's swimwear is limited and ranges from classic Speedos to tiger-print Versace – both equally awkward on the wrong physique. A much safer option is to go for classic surfer shorts. Quicksilver and Mambo are good choices for teens and twentysomethings, and Hackett offers more grown-up styles. But the best quality swimming trunks are at Vilebrequin, which has shops in St Tropez where it first started, as well as London and New York and offers six different shapes, ranging from its long Okoa style to the boxer-short shaped Moorea. They come in 80 designs from colourful modern renditions of Hawaiian prints and sea horses to classic checks. Guaranteed not to get you laughed off the beach.

Vilebrequin

Bra

Cadolle's Cara

Where?
255 Rue Saint Honoré, 75001, Paris, France • 00 33 1 42 60 94 94 • www.cadolle.com

How much?
Approx £530/$800/€600

One simply *must* buy one's underwear in Paris, the land of lovers and the location of the world's largest lingerie department, found in Galeries Lafayette. French women understand the importance of good underwear, that it gives you confidence, makes you feel super-sexy and ready to conquer the world. And nothing is more important than a bra that fits properly – a good one should change the appearance of your entire upper body. Alice Cadolle offers a unique made-to-measure bra service. Famous clients have included the legendary double agent Mata Hari, for whom a metal bra was created, Coco Chanel, who requested a chest-flattening design, as well as Catherine Deneuve, Brigitte Bardot and Christina Onassis. The *atelier* is located at the end of a courtyard, near the Hotel Costes, and looks like a scene straight out of the classic Audrey Hepburn movie *Funny Face* – think red velvet curtains and assistants with tape measures strewn around their necks. The boutique is now

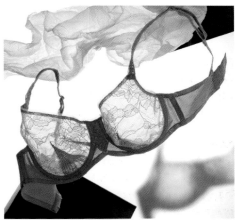

Cadolle's Cara brassiere

run by Poupie – her great-great grandmother was the inventor of the bra and her mother, Alice, became famous for her made-to-measure skills. Poupie has retained the company's heritage, as well as its devotion to quality, and her loyal customers come from all over the world. 'The English love eccentricity while the French love tradition and good taste,' she explains. 'Americans are very boring – they just want nude.'

The Cara, an everyday bra, is Poupie's attempt to reverse the trend for round, tennis-ball breasts, an unnatural shape born from the boom in plastic surgery. 'I want to reinvent the bra and create the perfect bust,' she explains. With the Cara, the breasts point from the bottom up and the back is low for support. 'The back needs to be low so the front goes up. You need rigid seams and rigid straps. I only use elastic at the back… Seamless bras don't support – they're a killer. In ten years time, my clients will be the women who've been wearing seamless bras!'

At least two fittings are required over a six-week period, and Poupie can conjure up whatever a client desires. Silk is the least effective fabric for a bra, nylon netting the best, and Cadolle has 60 different shades to choose from and 50 different types of lace. 'Skin colour is so unsexy, but it's the most popular.'

LA PERLA

Where? Stores worldwide including 163 Sloane Street, London, SW1 • 00 44 207 245 0527 • www.laperla.com

How much? Approx £145/$210/€154

The Italian luxury label is best for decorating smaller breasts. Think sexy lace and elegant silk fabrics – its Venus Allure range is especially covetable. It's little wonder that men make up around a third of all La Perla's customers.

WACOAL

Where? www.figleaves.com and stockists worldwide • see www.wacoal.co.uk

How much? From £30/$43/€32

For more than 50 years, Wacoal has specialized in perfecting the art of a great-fitting bra. The company's emphasis is on shape and proportion, whether it be a fantastic-working (and sexy-looking) minimizing bra or padding for the more petite. Bigger bosoms, in particular, find Wacoal's bras a godsend.

BRASSIERE BASICS

Rigby & Peller, corsetières to the Queen, are famous for their crack squad of fitters, who can tell the size of a woman's bra just by looking at her breasts, and are known to refuse to sell ill-fitting bras.

Jill Kenton of Rigby & Peller says: 'Around 75 percent of all women are wearing the wrong size bra. Walking down the street I see so many women whose breasts hang too low – this seems the most common problem. Whatever you may have heard, it's impossible to work out your bra size at home using a tape measure. Instead, go for a professional fitting at a reputable lingerie store and try on as many different styles as possible. The perfect bra should be snug around the ribcage. If it's too big round the back, the breasts are too low; too small round the cup, you will have four bosoms instead of two; too small around the back and it will hurt. The right bra should run in one line around your body. The underwiring should lie behind the breast tissue, almost under the armpit. 'One way of checking if your bra fits is to do the finger test: place your index finger under your bra and run it round your body. If your bra starts riding up, the size is too big.

'Some women blame falling straps on sloping shoulders. Again, this is a sign of an ill-fitting bra. A good bra should never fall off the shoulders. Many women's bra sizes fluctuate during the month. I recommend getting different bra sizes for different periods – if you value your breasts and don't want them to sag, this is a wise investment.

'Also, women should never wear wires while pregnant as their breasts are continually growing. The bra needs to be able to grow with the breast tissue – underwiring prevents this. Bras have a life of around two years and need to be handwashed. After that, throw them away!'

Rigby & Peller, 22A Conduit St, London, W1 and branches, www.rigbyandpeller.com.

The Alondra range from Rigby & Peller

Rigby & Peller

Cashmere sweater

Loro Piana

Where?

153 New Bond Street, W1 • 00 44
207 499 9300 •
821 Madison Avenue, New York, NY
10021 • 00 1 212 980 7961 •
www.loropiana.com

How much?

Approx £465/$700/€530

Loro Piana is cashmere's holy grail. It is the very best money can buy, and the label every aficionado worth their Ralph Lauren cable-knit (another classic) aspires to. If only it weren't so darned expensive. Yet with Loro Piana, feeling really is believing – the eyebrow-rising prices are the result of Loro Piana's stringent quality control. The company only uses the purest white cashmere, the most rare and therefore the most covetable, from the Kyo goat, which is found in remote high-altitude regions of Central Asia. The higher the altitude, the finer the yarn – or so the theory goes.

The Italian family firm was started in the 18th century in Quarona, in the Piemont region of northern Italy, where the headquarters are still based today, and it is now run by two very dapper brothers, Pier Luigi and Sergio Loro Piana.

As well as its own-brand collection – the company's wraps and men's suits also come highly recommended – and bespoke service, Loro Piana is the world's largest cashmere producer and supplies fabric for labels as diverse as Jil Sander, Giorgio Armani and J. Crew.

Loro Piana V-neck sweater

Lucien Pellat-Finet

PRINGLE V-NECK SWEATER

Where? 112 New Bond Street, London, W1 • 00 44 207 297 4580 • www.pringlescotland.com • stockists worldwide

How much? Prices from approx £225/$340/€255 Pringle's trademark – a rampant Scottish lion – is recognizable throughout the world, and the label was the one that stylish stars of the 1950s, such as Grace Kelly and Lauren Bacall, turned to for their twin sets. Founded in 1815 by Robert Pringle, the brand has been revamped in recent years and today has a fresher, more fashionable image.

LUCIEN PELLAT-FINET SWEATER

Where? 1 Rue de Montalembert, 75007, Paris, France • 00 33 1 42 22 22 77 • www.lucienpellat-finet.com

How much? From £1,150/$1,730/€1,300 A Lucien Pellat-Finet sweater screams Euroluxe and is much more exciting than a standard black roll-neck. Worth every penny for the wow factor and top-notch craftsmanship, these sweaters sport psychedelic colours and unusual motifs – think skulls, medals and marijuana leaves.

' I vividly remember the first time I paid thousands of dollars for cashmere. It was ten years ago in LA and I bought a lilac Lucien Pellat Finet sweater with a huge green marijuana leaf on it from Fred Segal. It cost me $2,800 and it was the ultimate in f**k-you glamour. Since then I've collected them – I bought the tiger print one, the leopard print one and the skull one. I buy a couple a year – I must have at least 20 by now. I love the fact they are luxurious but have a sense of humour. I don't want to be walking around in beige or taupe cashmere – I'll leave that to someone else!

'What I love about cashmere is that it breathes – it keeps you warm when it's cold but you can also wear it to the beach so it's great for travelling. It's the ultimate in relaxed chic – you can just sling it on over a thin T-shirt or wear it directly against your skin. You can't do that with lambswool.'

Patrick Cox, London-based shoe designer, on why he loves Lucien Pellat-Finet

The Best High-Street Cashmere

Where? Uniqlo • Branches worldwide • www.uniqlo.co.uk

How much? From £39/$77/€57

Thanks to mass-production in China, cashmere – once the apogee of sartorial luxury – is now affordable for everyone. But with one regrettable downside: quality. In recent consumer tests, garments that promised '100 percent cashmere' actually contained camel hair and – horror of horrors! – wool, a sneaky trick that partly explains why high-street cashmere never feels quite as nice as the pricier stuff (and bobbles in the blink of an eye). Still, we're smitten, and the best we've found is from Uniqlo, the Japanese budget chain that excels in great-fitting cashmere separates – from classic V-necks to long-length cardies – in a fantastic range of colours. So popular are Uniqlo's cashmeres, in fact, that last year in the run-up to Christmas the brand opened a temporary cashmere-only shop in London to keep up with the demand. It is worth remembering, though, that cheap cashmere pieces will never last as long as garments made in Italy or Scotland. With cashmere, you really do get what you pay for.

Coat for men

Gieves & Hawkes

Where?
www.gievesandhawkes.com
How much?
From £700 /$1000/€752

Based at one of London's smartest addresses – no. 1 Savile Row – this British label dates back to 1771. With a history of producing fine military attire, Gieves & Hawkes' contemporary designs utilize the brand's rich heritage; its recent coat designs have included biker, trench and woollen pea coats.

GLOVERALL

Where? www.gloverall.com •
www.doverstreetmarket.com
How much? From £179/$253/€193
No other coat says warmth, comfort and durability like the duffle coat. And no one produces better than Gloverall, who have been going strong since 1951, when their first factory was situated behind St Paul's cathedral in London. The classic duffles are still made by skilled machinists with decades of experience and have recently garnered a new generation of street-savvy wearers – they are even stocked at London emporium of cool, Dover Street Market.

MONCLER

Where? www.moncler.com
How much? £250/$358/€269
This ultra-stylish Italian label has been providing snappy quilted jackets since it launched in 1954. Its signature garment is the shiny, quilted ski jacket adorned by Olympic skiers and the impeccably dressed skiing school of St Moritz. Moncler has recently found its way from the Alpine slopes to the chic streets of Paris, Milan and even London.

Gieves & Hawkes

Coat for women

MaxMara

Where?
Stores worldwide including MaxMara, 19–21 Old Bond Street,
London, W1 • 00 44 20 7499 7902
How much?
From approx £600/$850/€649

Italians know how to wrap-up in style. When they are looking
for an everyday winter coat, the first place they turn to is
MaxMara. Actually, over 10,000 women a season worldwide
buy a classic MaxMara camel coat. Cate Blanchett was wearing
a cream cashmere-style when she married, and Ingrid Bergman
bought one for her daughter Isabella Rossellini as a coming-of-
age present. It's no wonder these coats are so popular, as
the brand, established by Achille Maramotti in 1947, produces
the most timeless, grown-up and value-for-money coats
around. Impeccably-cut, each MaxMara coat goes through a
mighty 73 stages of production. Its double breasted camel
cashmere coat, originally launched in 1983, remains one of its
best-selling styles. Look after it well, and it will be an
investment for decades.

AQUASCUTUM
Where? Stores worldwide including 100 Regent St, London,
W1 • 00 44 20 7675 8200 • www.aquascutum.com
How much? From approx £600/$850/€649
The most influential British coat-maker of the 20th century
continues to provide classic, quality woollen coats with plenty
of neat belted-styles each season. Made from a variety of
durable natural fabrics, Aquascutum coats are guaranteed to
keep you snug.

WHISTLES
Where? High streets nationwide in the UK •
www.whistles.co.uk
How much? From approx £195/$278/€211
Come rain or shine, this British high-street stalwart produces
chic, well-made coats at very affordable prices. Timeless styles
such as pea coats, belted trenches and funnel necks have all
been recent hits.

MaxMara

Jeans for men

APC

Where?
www.my-wardrobe.com • www.apc.fr

How much?
From £101/$144/€130

French man Jean Touitou set up his label APC (*Atelier de Production et de Création*) in 1987. It has been an underground hit ever since with legions of fans hooked on its simple, streamline jeans in quality Japanese denims. Its straight-fitting 'New Standard' shape made in selvage denim and featuring those all important red stripes on the inside leg is a current must-have for fashion-savvy men around the world.

APC jeans

ACNE
Where? www.acnestudios.com
How much? From approx £150/$214/€161
Standing for 'Ambition to Create Novel Experience', Acne, the cult Swedish brand, was established in 1996. Since then, it has garnered a loyal fan base keen on its slim aesthetic and cool street credentials. The label has recently collaborated with one of the world's most luxurious brands, Lanvin, for a small and hugely desirable capsule range.

EDWIN
Where? www.thecorner.com • www.edwin-europe.com
How much? From £150/$214/€161
Edwin (an anagram of denim with an upside-down 'm') is a hard-to-come-by brand, specializing in covetable dark Japanese denim jeans in a signature slim-fit. Its exclusivity only adds to its desirability.

Acne jeans

THE DEVIL'S IN THE DETAIL
You can tell a lot about the quality of a pair of jeans by looking at the details. The **selvage** is the white stripe running down the seam, which seals the edge of the denim to prevent it fraying – experts can tell the brand and quality of the denim just by looking at this; New Yorkers actually show them off by rolling their jeans up. **Rivets** are the little metal studs used to reinforce the pockets and prevent wear and fraying. The **rise** is the distance between the crotch and the waistband. In many ways, the **back pocket** is now more important than the cut – it's the telltale sign of the brand and the position is instrumental in flattering the bottom. **Washes** are getting ever more complex; the older and more worn your jeans look, whether through sandblasting, rock washing or punching with holes, the more expensive they are likely to be.

CULT CLASSIC: LEVI'S 501S

Who hasn't owned a pair of trusty old Levi's 501s at some point? They are, without doubt, the most classic and iconic jeans ever and while not exactly the height of fashion, Levi's 501 will probably be around for much longer than many of the flashy young jeans currently on the market.

Levi Strauss was a Jewish Bavarian immigrant who hooked up with tailor Jacob Davis in San Francisco to create men's trousers that wouldn't rip. Jacob had the brainwave of introducing rivets at points of strain, such as the pocket corners and base of the button fly. Although denim originates from 17th century France, and American men had worn denim trousers without rivets for much of the 19th century, 1873 – the year Levi Strauss & Co. patented denim jeans with rivets – is viewed as the official birth date of blue jeans.

The number 501 was assigned to the jeans in 1890 and the red tab was later added in 1936 to help identify them from a distance. The double row stitching on the back pockets, known as the Arcuate stitching design, is the oldest apparel trademark still in use today; it was first used in 1873 and during the Second World War,

when it was painted on the pockets due to government rationing of essential items such as thread. Since 1966, reinforced stitching has replaced the back pocket rivets.

A Levi's red tab with a capital E indicates they were made pre-1971. Levi's bought a pair of 1890 501s for $25,000 (£17,120) in 1997. Today, a typical pair of 501s takes 3 metres (3¼ yards) of denim, five buttons, six rivets and 37 separate sewing operations.

Jeans for women

Earnest Sewn

Where?

821 Washington Street, New York, NY 10014
• 00 1 212 242 3414 • www.earnestsewn.com •
Selfridges, 400 Oxford Street, London, W1, and
branches • 00 44 800 123 400

How much?

From £150/$230/€170

Earnest Sewn Harlan

What is it about jeans? They're so simple, yet so desirable; they are both everyday and the height of glamour, gliding from the office to the cocktail bar with just a few accessory changes. In fact, denim is now so alluring that we live in an age when it's not unusual to part with £150 for a pair of jeans – make that £400 if you want made-to-measure.

But which jeans are the most coveted of them all? Like perfume and bikinis, buying jeans is a highly personal affair – different brands and shapes suit different people. However, there are some jeans that are guaranteed to fulfil all desires. These are the styles and brands that shine above the rest in terms of quality, fit and wash.

A few years ago, New York-based Scott Morrison, former co-founder/ designer of Paper Denim & Cloth, set about trying to establish the finest jeans brand in the world. The result was Earnest Cut & Sew. Fusing the garment's American workwear origins with the ancient Japanese style asthetic 'wabi sabi' (the idea of beauty in irregularity), the range includes high-quality denim and superior cuts. And if you're not taken with the luscious cigarette-style slim jeans, you can get your very own pair made-to-measure, a service available at the New York store, Barneys, and at Selfridges, London, where you decide which cut, buttons, rivets, thread colour and back pocket you would like. The quest for the perfect jeans might just be over.

Citizens of Humanity Kelly Bootcut

CITIZENS OF HUMANITY

Where? www.citizensofhumanity.com

How much? £72/$141/€107

Created by Jerome Dahan, formerly of Seven, Citizens of Humanity's jeans have a low-rise waistband, but not too low, and are accommodating around the hips, thighs and bottom, making the legs seem miraculously thinner. Recent styles have included a slightly wider leg, in-line with the more flared new direction of jeans.

7 FOR ALL MANKIND

Where? www.7forallmankind.com • Department stores including Selfridges

How much? From approx £150/$230/€170

When Seven jeans burst onto the scene in 2000, they became an instant hit, due to the remarkably slimming cut. Now, despite numerous new competitors, Seven jeans, with 'For All Mankind' added to the moniker, remain desirable thanks to the simple, flattering silhouette and deep-blue washes.

> *' I wish I had invented blue jeans... Jeans are expressive and discreet, they have sex appeal and simplicity – everything I could want for the clothes I design.'*
>
> **Yves Saint Laurent, fashion designer**

> *' Jeans are your most important piece of clothing, no question. They have to be worn. And they've got to be old. I also prefer that they be button-fly. The right jeans and a T-shirt can be sexier than the most expensive tailored suit.'*
>
> **Donna Karan, fashion designer**

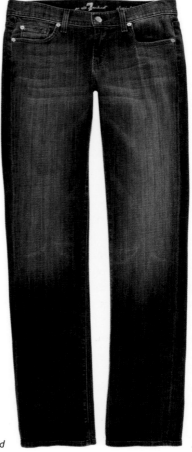

7 For All Mankind

The best...

Skinny jeans are by Acne, J Brand and Superfine. They're good on lean and gamine types. Available at boutiques, including www.brownsfashion.com

White jeans are by James Jeans – the Sammy White Pearl rocks and is surprisingly flattering. Available at www.shopbop.com and www.jamesjeans.us

Cropped jeans are by Citizens of Humanity – the cropped 'Kelly' stretch is the style to seek out. Available at Selfridges.

All-round flattering jeans are Paige Denim's Laurel Canyon five-pocket stretch, thanks to lean styling, a permanent crease at the front and well-placed pockets. For stockists see www.paigepremiumdenim.com

Sassy LA jeans are by Serfontaine, Blue Cult, Goldsign and Juicy Couture, and are excellent for curvy girls. Available at Harvey Nichols and Selfridges.

Rock and roll cool jeans are by True Religion due to their slouchy fit, funky pocket stitching and distressed detailing. Available at www.truereligionbrandjeans.com

Deconstructed jeans with a modern edge are by Ødyn, a relatively new Swedish brand that offers a fresh look and is a nice antidote to all those LA brands. Available at www.revolveclothing.com and www.odynjeans.com

---

Knickers

Agent Provocateur

Where?

6 Broadwick Street, London, W1 and branches • 00 44 207 439 0229 • www.agentprovocateur.com

How much?

From approx £40/$60/€45

This super-cool London label made it acceptable for British women to spend upwards of £20 on a pair of panties when it was first launched by Joe Corre and Serena Rees in 1994. The range, which now includes a seductive bridal collection and maternity line, is famous for its flirty designs served up by assistants in appropriately provocative pink mini-dresses.

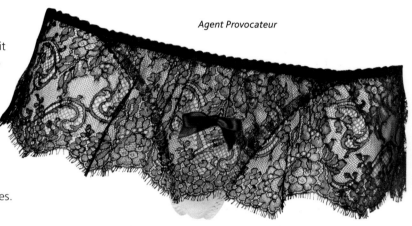

Agent Provocateur

SABBIA ROSA

Where? 71–73 Rue des Saints-Pères, 75006, Paris, France • 00 33 1 45 48 8 37
How much? From approx £132/$199/€150
A pair of knickers is by far the most personal and thrilling purchase a woman can make. Madame Sabbia Rosa's elegant lingerie boutique in Saint-Germain-des-Prés in Paris sells the finest French silk in a rainbow of sherbet shades. Her exquisite hand-made silk smalls have attracted the world's best dressed and wealthiest women, including Sofia Coppola, Kate Moss and Catherine Deneuve. Naomi Campbell loves Sabbia Rosa's knickers so much she's been known to buy up the entire collection in one go.

LA PERLA

Where? 163 Sloane Street, London, SW1 • 00 44 207 245 0527 • www.laperla.com • Stores worldwide
How much? From about approx £30/$55/€45
The Italian brand synonymous with sex-appeal makes knickers in top-quality lace and pleated tulle. Styles have a screen-star appeal in sexy black or more neutral beiges and creams.

The world's most comfortable pants

If it is simply a fabulously flattering pair of pants you're after, the kind that won't expose any lumps and bumps or peep above the waistband of jeans and skirts, we have three recommendations. **Cosabella** (www.cosabella.com) is an Italian brand that produces the archetypal knicker shape in sheer colours, while **Elle Macpherson Intimates** (www.ellemacphersonintimates.com) do a fantastic low-slung range that flatters the figure no end. British company **Bodas** (www.bodas.co.uk) also offers an excellent range of neutrally toned knickers with minimal seams to prevent the dreaded VPL.

Little black dress

Lanvin

Where?
22 Rue du Fauborg St-Honoré, 75008, Paris, France • 00 33 1 44 71 31 73 • 128 Mount Street, London, W1 • 00 44 207 494 4786 • www.lanvin.com

How much?
From £858/$1,684/€1,279

Lanvin

Jeanne Lanvin set up as a milliner in Paris in 1889 and went on to become one of the leading female couturiers of the early 19th century, her name synonymous with a pure, feminine style. Lanvin excelled at designing beautiful dresses for mothers and daughters and was known for the 'robe de style': a dress with a dropped waist and full skirt. Fast-forward to the next century and Israeli designer Alber Elbaz has revived the label's appeal – albeit with a dash of urban modernity – in his role as artistic director. This award-winning designer studied at the Tel Aviv School of Fashion and Textiles, trained in New York under the watchful eye of society-couturier, Geoffrey Beene, and made his name as artistic director at Yves Saint Laurent in 1998. He has proved, just like Jeanne Lanvin, that he has an instinct for creating divine dresses and, most importantly, the ultimate little black dress. His flattering, cinch-waist LBDs, a favourite with the red carpet contingent, appear effortless, and fit the female form to perfection.

CHANEL
Where? Chanel stores worldwide • www.chanel.com
How much? Approx £2,000/$3,000/€2,275
Karl Lagerfeld keeps the spirit of Coco Chanel and the LBD heritage alive (*see box opposite*) by designing around six new styles each season from simple shifts to body-skimming gowns. A Chanel LBD is an investment for life.

VANESSA BRUNO
Where? www.net-a-porter.com • www.vanessabruno.com
How much? From approx £200/$285/€215
Since launching her chic ready-to-wear label in the 1990s, Parisian Vanessa Bruno has proved she has a natural instinct when it comes to dressing women. Each season, her collection includes a range of highly wearable little black dresses with a twist, in signature slinky fabrics, such as silk and jersey.

Chanel

Vanessa Bruno

'***A*** dress can be the expression of a state of mind. There are dresses that sing of joy of life, dresses that weep, dresses that threaten. There are gay dresses, mysterious dresses, pleasing dresses and tearful dresses.'

Paul Poiret, designer, 1879–1944

THE ORIGINS OF THE LITTLE BLACK DRESS

In 1919, Coco Chanel put black in fashion. Seven years later, *American Vogue* illustrated the Chanel 'Ford', calling it the 'frock that all the world would wear'. It was a sleeveless, black crepe-de-chine dress with a pin-tucked front, and thus the little black dress was born. Many have evolved the look. In the 1950s, French couturier, Jacques Fath, created elegant dresses to flatter the hourglass figure; in the 1960s, the LBD became truly fashionable once more with the mini-dress, epitomized by Twiggy and the designer Paco Rabanne. In the late 1960s and 1970s,

British designer Jean Muir made the 'little nothing' of a black dress a classic. As she said: 'When you have found something that suits you and never lets you down, why not stick to it?' Now, it is not only Karl Lagerfeld, Alber Elbaz and Diane von Furstenberg who are pushing the LBD into the 21st century with style and grace, but also a new generation of dress designers including Georgina Chapman and Kerin Craig for the A-lister's favourite Marchesa (available at www.neimanmarcus.com), and Narciso Rodriquez (available at www.net-a-porter.com). Long may it live.

Pyjamas

Derek Rose

Where?
www.derek-rose.com • 00 44 845
602 0745

How much?
From approx £110/$165/€125

Derek Rose

We're currently in the grip of a pyjama boom. Thanks to the recent trend for 'relaxation' gear coupled with men rediscovering the joys of nightwear, sales have risen by over 20 percent. Derek Rose is the undisputed king of 'pjs'. His collection is worn by everyone from the Queen to the children at Hogwarts in the 'Harry Potter' films – even John and Yoko had matching his-and-hers pairs.

The Savile Row company, which was founded in 1926, specializes in tailored pyjamas – a flattering and generous cut, an elasticated waist, and a draught-proof array of buttons – in essence everything you could want from the perfect pyjama. The blue satin stripe with a single pocket and white piping is their bestseller, and since the company started a woman's line, the pink satin stripe is doing a roaring trade, too. The key is Rose's insistence that the satin is made from two-fold yarn, which gives the cloth more depth as well as ensuring it lasts longer. Also popular are the company's silk designs – *very* Cary Grant – as well as the military-influenced Regimental Stripe collection: with names like Black Watch and Brigade of Guards. A good pair of pjs is essential. After all, at some point everyone ends up a weekend guest – and 4am visits to the bathroom in a faded Snoopy T-shirt just won't do.

LAURENCE TAVERNIER
Where? 32 Rue du Bac, 75007, Paris, France • 00 33 1 49 27 01 69 • www.laurencetavernier.com
How much? From approx £140/$210/€159
This French luxury label is dedicated to nightwear, making soft, cotton pyjamas, which are surprisingly elegant, yet still comfortable, as well as woollen bed coats, cashmere robes, slippers and bed socks. A range that is chic enough to wear outside the house.

BROOKS BROTHERS
Where? Liberty Plaza, One Liberty Plaza, New York, NY 10006 • 00 1 212 267 2400 • 150 Regent Street, London, W1 • 00 44 207 238 0030 • www.brooksbrothers.com
How much? From approx £69/$65/€78
Brooks Brothers' candy-stripe pyjamas are the ones Madonna wore when photographed at home in bed with her children – in matching pairs – for *US Vogue*. Perfectly preppy, they're made from soft cotton with a darker blue piping and a drawstring waist.

Raincoat

Burberry trenchcoat

Where?
21–23 New Bond Street, London, W1 • 00 44 207 968 0000 • www.burberry.com

How much?
From approx £395/$600/€450

It's hard to pinpoint exactly what makes the Burberry trenchcoat such a timeless classic. The hint of checked lining, perhaps? The simple belted form? The smart military epaulettes? In the early 1900s, army officers started wearing these coats as part of their uniform and, by the 1940s, the trenchcoat had filtered into mainstream fashion. Today, the Burberry trench is still made from a closely woven Egyptian cotton called gabardine. It remains the best-loved raincoat there is, with all its authentic details still intact, such as the metal D-rings on the belt. Burberry's current Creative Director, Christopher Bailey, updates the style each season, reviving it with long or short hemlines, in a variety of colours and fabrics, including luxurious leather, suede and tweed. For the ultimate raincoat, you can now get your own bespoke Burberry trench, made up to your specific shape and size. You can even get your intials embroidered onto the lining.

Burberry trenchcoat

MACKINTOSH

Where? 54–55 Burlington Arcade, London, W1 • 00 44 207 529 5950 • www.mackintoshwear.com
How much? From £495/$885/€725
Created in the late 19th century, Mackintosh is the original waterproof coat, made from a waterproof woollen fabric that was patented in 1829 by Charles Mackintosh and Charles Goodyear. The classic British company now offers a made-to-measure service at the flagship London store.

AQUASCUTUM

Where? 100 Regent Street, London, W1 • 00 44 207 675 8200 • www.aquascutum.com
How much? From £525/$795/€600
In 1851, John Emary opened a small, high-quality tailors shop on Regent Street and in 1883 created the first rain-repellent cloth, naming it Aquascutum, from the Latin for 'water' and 'shield', which subsequently became the name of his clothing brand. Emary went on to make a coat for King Edward VII in the late 1890s before creating trenchcoats for soldiers – and Winston Churchill. The contemporary Aquascutum range includes modern takes on the classic trench, but if it's a traditional style you're after, go for the classic Kingsgate design, available in navy, dark beige and black.

Shirt for men

Where?
28 Place Vendôme, 75001, Paris,
France • 00 33 1 42 60 30 70

How much?
Bespoke shirts from approx
£370/$560/€420

Housed in an elegant seven-floor building in Paris' Place Vendôme, Charvet is ground zero for shirt aficionados. Apart from the fact that it is reputed to have the largest selection of shirt fabrics in the world – they have 400 different shades of white and at least 200 different blues to choose from – the cut is impeccable. With its squared-off bottom, smart collar, elegant cuffs and solid buttons, a Charvet shirt looks as good with a bespoke suit as it does under a lambswool V-neck sweater.

TURNBULL & ASSER

Where? 71–72 Jermyn Street, London, SW1 • 00 44 207 808 3000 • www.turnbullandasser.com

How much? From £165/$250/€190: minimum of six shirts for first order. Worn by prime ministers and princes

Charvet's fine cotton shirts

alike (it is rumoured that the Sultan of Oman ordered 240 shirts in 20 minutes), this renowned British label was established in 1885 and offers the highest-quality shirts you can find in the UK. Choose from 1,000 different cloths, ranging from plain white poplin to voile, and brushed cotton to silk. What sets these shirts apart from the competition is the classic deep-spread collar, three-button barrel cuff, white lining and deep mother of pearl buttons.

SIMONE ABBARCHI

Where? Borgo Santissimi Apostoli 16, Borgo Santissimi, Florence, Italy • 00 39 055 210 552

How much? From approx £90/$135/€100

The Italian tailor makes 3,000 shirts a year and has a loyal client base from London to LA. Customers start with a 25-minute consultation, during which measurements are taken and sample swatches shown. All the shirts are made exclusively from Italian cotton, linen, and silk.

Shirt for women

Thomas Pink

Where?
Branches worldwide • online at www.thomaspink.com

How much?
From £69/$100/€74

Thomas Pink

When Audrey Hepburn raced across a piazza wearing a fitted white shirt in the 1953 film *Roman Holiday*, a sartorial classic was born. The white shirt quickly became synonymous with all that is fresh and playful despite the work-a-day ethic behind its origins. Worn the right way – dressed down, with a simple pair of blue jeans, or dressed up, with a full-length evening skirt and costume jewellery, it's amazing how something so simple can still turn heads.

Nowadays there are endless variations on the white shirt. The Brazilian designer Anne Fontaine, for instance, has built an entire business on the white shirt, with 100 new styles each season. And the price varies too, with everything from bargain-basement transparent horrors to shirts costing £300 a pop from Daphne Guinness' covetable capsule collection at Dover Street Market in London.

But we believe part of the power of the white shirt is in its crispness, and that requires it to be box-fresh (or as close as possible). Which means there is little point in spending a fortune. As well as sparkling clean, the perfect white shirt should also be fitted – not tight, not baggy – and made from pure cotton (or perhaps, for evening, silk). And that's it. As the endlessly elegant designer Carolina Herrera, who has been wearing a signature white shirt all her life, explains: 'It is about simplicity – they don't look complicated – it has to look effortless.'

Thomas Pink produces the best white shirts we've found in good-quality fabrics that include twill, poplin and Sea Island Cotton. If the women's styles are not to your taste – some women prefer a more masculine style with no front darts – then head to the men's section, roll up your sleeves, and perfect that morning-after look. Thomas Pink also has a made-to-measure service. For a cheaper white shirt fix, go to Gap or, better still, one of H&M's branches of COS (www.cosstores.com), which has a fantastic selection of pure cotton shirts in fashion-forward shapes.

BROOKS BROTHERS

Where? Stores nationwide • www.brooksbrothers.com
How much? £61/$89.50/€66

When Oprah – a long-time white-shirt fan – recently declared Brooks Brothers' non-iron range her favourite, all 23,000 shirts sold out in two days. Dubbed 'the miracle shirt', it is pure cotton with a special treatment to help it remain crease-free.

VIKTOR & ROLF

Where? From boutiques worldwide • www.viktor-rolf.com
How much? From £150/$218/€160

And, if you *do* fancy splurging on a truly special white shirt, then Dutch design duo Viktor & Rolf offer the best variations, from bows and exquisite embroidery to shirts with oversized collars. Always sharp and never frou-frou.

Tie

Hermès

Where?
Hermès stores worldwide • www.hermes.com

How much?
From approx £107/$160/€120

The tie: a curious invention and not entirely necessary. Well, it doesn't exactly serve much practical purpose, now, does it? The thing is, a shirt can look somewhat vacant without one. A shirt and tie form an important sartorial partnership, and matching a shirt colour and pattern to the tie is essential. So, too, is the way a collar sits on the neck – it should be neither too low nor too high – the way the knot fills the spread (so that it isn't too fat or too skinny) and the way in which the blade covers the placket of the shirt front to finish on the waistband. Then there's the texture: the perfect tie should be good to the touch – neither too floppy nor too rigid, but in a weighty, quality silk.

The classic Hermès tie is, for men, what their silk scarves are for women: refined, traditional and superior in quality. That discreet green and orange 'Hermès' label on the back is loaded with meaning – suggesting expense, refinement and wealth. The designs are classic with a twist and guaranteed to carry weight in the boardroom.

Hermès' classic ties

DRAKES

Where? Select menswear boutiques throughout Europe • www.drakes-london.com
How much? Approx £85/$120/€91
Founded in 1977, Drakes is now the largest independent producer of handmade ties in England. The classic designs, lovingly handmade in a family-run factory in East London, appeal to the conservative dressers of Milan, Paris and Vienna as much as the street-savvy Londoner.

EMILIO PUCCI

Where? 170 Sloane Street, London, SW1 • 00 44 207 221 8171
• www.pucci.com
How much? From £80/$120/€90
Vibrant Italian brand, Emilio Pucci, still designs some of the most iconic of ties in its signature swirly prints. Bold, bright and a flamboyant style statement in their own right. Search on eBay for classic and collectible 1960s' styles.

Drakes

T-shirt for men

Albam

Where?
23 Beak Street, London, W1 •
00 44 20 3157 7000 •
www.albamclothing.com

How much?
From £25/$36/€27

Albam

The plain and simple T-shirt is probably the most widely worn garment in the world. So you would have thought it would be a cinch to find a good one – one that works in a variety of contexts and fits in all the right places – but it's not. For men, a T-shirt should neither be too baggy nor too tight. Ideally, you want it to hint at those sculpted pecks and leave the rest to the imagination.

This independent London-run company specializes in producing small runs of quality products, so it can offer them at affordable prices. Its 'Classic T', made from luxury Egyptian cotton, is perfectly proportioned and is produced in either a crew- or a V-neck.

T-shirts in every colour at American Apparel

AMERICAN APPAREL

Where? American Apparel stores worldwide •
www.americanapparel.net

How much? From £13/$17/€17

This US T-shirt label's 2001 version of the fine, jersey short-sleeved classic T-shirt is slightly fitted and of a soft texture. Best of all, the label is anti-sweatshops. The ethical consumer's choice.

HANES

Where? Department stores worldwide •
00 1 800 254 1545 • www.hanes.com

How much? From £6/$9/€6

As worn by Marlon Brando, this classic American T-shirt brand's short-sleeved 'Beefy T' in white features 100 percent ringspun cotton, high-stitch density fabric and double-needled seams.

T-shirt for women

C&C California

Where?
Selected department stores worldwide, including Barneys, Bergdorf Goodman, Saks, Harvey Nichols and Selfridges • www.candccalifornia.com

How much?
From £32/$48/€36

C&C California's 'Classic Tee'

The perfect T-shirt for a woman is one that covers the midriff and skims the top of the jeans with a fit that shows you have breasts without turning you into a contestant from a wet T-shirt competition. Sleeves are vital, too – you don't want them to be too square and long, or you'll look like a throwback from an 80s' pop band; and you don't want a capped sleeve, as that's not a T-shirt at all.

C&C California was founded by Los Angeles-based design duo Cheyann Benedict and Claire Stansfield in 2003. Their mission was to create the best T-shirt ever – and they've succeeded with flying colours. Each of the 20 styles is made from ultra-fine combed cotton, so it moves and stretches in all the right ways while feeling ultra-soft on the skin. There are now over 50 colours to choose from, with more being added all the time.

C&C's most perfect T-shirt is the 'Classic Tee', which features a flattering, wider-than-usual crewneck, and also provides the perfect coverage over low-slung jeans. Lightweight and luxurious against the skin, it can be worn alone or layered beneath another. A wardrobe staple.

PETIT BATEAU
Where? Petit Bateau stores worldwide • www.petit-bateau.com
How much? From £13/$22/€27
The classic French kidswear label, set up in 1893, Petit Bateau's short-sleeved, scalloped crewneck T-shirt is as plain and simple as can be, with a classic cut and quality, thick cotton.

JAMES PERSE
Where? www.jamesperse.com
How much? Approx £35/$50/€37
James Perse's eponymous LA label produces some of the coolest T-shirts we've found, in fine-gauge cottons and linens. Pick from seductive scoop neck cuts to casual V-necks.

Wedding dress

Vera Wang

Vera Wang:
Fairy Dust

Where?
Vera Wang Bridal Salon, Selfridges, 400 Oxford Street, London, W1
• 00 44 800 123 400 • www.verawangonweddings.com

How much?
From approx £2,400/$3,600/€2,730

Since the early 1990s, Vera Wang has been the bridal label with the maximum kudos. Her dresses have a signature look, with clean lines and minimal fuss, yet they possess head-turning glamour. Wang treats the wedding aisle with the same attitude other designers treat the red carpet, and she has fittingly been the designer-of-choice for many an A-list bride – think Uma Thurman, Jessica Simpson and Sharon Stone – single-handedly forcing other more traditional wedding dressmakers to go back to the drawing board.

Frustrated at being unable to find a suitable dress for her own wedding, Wang spotted a niche in the market. In 1990, she opened her first boutique in the glitzy uptown Carlyle Hotel in New York. The collection was an instant hit, with brides-to-be swooning over the expensive fabrics and exquisite detailing such as delicate hand-sewn beading. More than anything, though, they lap up Wang's vision of the modern bride: a career woman, quite possibly older than brides of yore, looking for a suitably sophisticated and grown-up dress.

Vera Wang:
Bouquet

Vera Wang still has a showroom at the Carlyle, a space that's considered by many as the ultimate bridal salon. Since she now has so many imitators, all of her gowns come with a certificate of authenticity. Wang has also branched out into non-bridal clothes as well as perfume, but it is wedding dresses for which she will be forever known. Her Manhattan sample sales remain the stuff of legend – bridezillas have been known to travel across continents to fight tooth and claw for a heavily discounted gown, many of them one-of-a-kind.

MONIQUE LHUILLIER

Where? 8485 Melrose Place, Los Angeles 90069 • 001 323 655 1088 • www.moniquelhuillier.com

How much? From £2,000/$3,000/€2,300

Since starting her company in 1996, Monique Lhuillier's range of gowns – romantic, dreamy, with a subtle sexuality – has gone from strength to strength. Many have a long silk sash, adding a welcome splash of colour to the bridal outfit.

Stewart Parvin

STEWART PARVIN

Where? 14 Motcomb Street, London, SW1 • 00 44 207 235 1125 • www.stewartparvin.com

How much? From £1,800/$2,700/€2,000 for a dress from the white label line • From £4,000/$6,000/€4,500 for a bespoke dress from the black label line

As one of the Queen's favourite designers, Parvin's well-heeled clientele know they're getting quality. They are also getting timeless style; his designs are strong and structured with razor-sharp lines. There is both a bespoke and a diffusion line. Parvin's promise is a couture-looking gown, even if it's off the peg.

SARTORIAL TIPS FOR THE MERINGUE-A-PHOBIC BRIDE

Browns Bride (www.brownsfashion.com) is a bridal boutique with a difference. An outpost of the famous South Molton Street shop – which itself is internationally renowned for spotting up-and-coming designers – the philosophy behind Bride is no different. As well as elegant designs from Emanuel Ungaro, Badgley Mischka and Monique Lhuillier, the store stocks more fashion-forward designs: from peach, ruffled Marc Jacobs numbers (hardly the traditional bridal getup but endlessly pretty nonetheless) to the more avant-garde Comme des Garçons.

Here the boutique's owner, Caroline Burstein Collis, gives invaluable tips for the thoroughly modern bride...

• Registry-office weddings are a great chance to break the style rules. A stunning example could be a sexy cream Alexander McQueen fitted suit, worn with a pair of Louboutin patent platform shoes in a shade of 'skin'.

• It's probably best not to look overly sexy on your wedding day, but if you are a sensual woman, you will want to show off this strong side of your personality – and your fiancée will love you all the more for it. For those with a fabulous figure, an Azzadine Alaia piece will show off your curves and pull you in all the right places.

• Red is a wonderful alternative to the white wedding dress. Monique Lhuillier recently made a blood-red ball gown for one of our brides who married in Scotland at her fiancé's castle on New Year's Eve. They had snow and a sleigh to carry them away.

• Black is the other colour that a few 'alternative' brides go for. It is not for the faint-hearted, but I have seen it looking wonderful.

• Non-traditional names to look out for include Alberta Ferretti and Carlos Miele, who both create wedding dresses that are sensual and romantic. They are not traditional in any sense; instead, are soft and flowing with that 'wow' factor, and are perfect for destination weddings since they pack easily into a small suitcase.

• Last but not least, Browns' latest wedding dress innovation is the 'Emergency' wedding gown. It packs up into a roll, is made from silk jersey with a separate tulle underskirt, is crush-proof and comes with a bottle of black or red Dylon so you can dye it after the wedding and wear it again. Really, what could be more modern than that!

Food & drink

'Eating is not merely a material pleasure. Eating well gives a spectacular joy to life and contributes immensely to goodwill and happy companionship. It is of great importance to the morale.'

Elsa Schiaparelli, fashion designer, 1890–1973

Balsamic vinegar

Giuseppe Giusti Aceto Balsamico Tradizionale

Where?

Via Quattroville 155, 41100 Modena, Italy • 00 39 059 856 135 • www.giusti.it • Good delis and gourmet websites worldwide, including: www.deandeluca.com and www.clubsauce.com

How much?

From £11/£20/€16 up to £220/$335/€250

Giuseppe Giusti

It might seem surprising today, but balsamic vinegar wasn't on sale commercially until the 1960s. Before then, this 'black gold' was a well-kept secret, the sole preserve of Italian housewives lucky enough to know a decent producer. Nowadays, it is available in supermarkets all over the world, although for the most part it isn't actually balsamic vinegar; instead, it's a mixture of wine vinegar, caramel and colourings, a concoction that tastes astringent when compared to the real thing. Grapes should be the only ingredient.

The good stuff should be as dark as treacle and almost as thick, the taste a balance of sweet and sour. The general rule is the older the vinegar, the better. There are two key terms to look out for: *'tradizionale'*, which means it has been aged for at least 12 years, and 'DOC', meaning it comes from a controlled denomination. You also need to check the provenance, as proper balsamic vinegar can only come from Modena in Italy, where they have stringent rules, similar to the appellation system for wines in France. Wax stamps placed over the corks are colour-coded in relation to age: red and white for vinegars at least 12 years old, silver for at least 18 years old, and gold for 25 years or more. Particulary old and therefore high-quality vinegars will have a distinctive short and stocky bottle and stand.

You really can't go wrong with any aged balsamic vinegar from Modena. One of the oldest producers is Giusti, a family business that has been going since the early 17th century. The whole range is recommended, in particular their 40-year-old vintage, the perfect gift for any gourmand. Giusti's vinegar has been described as 'sweet, warm and wooded with a tart finish'. Buy from the family's Modena store, once frequented by the composer Giuseppe Verdi (1813–1901).

ACETAIA LEONARDI BALSAMICO
Where? Good international delis • www.acetaialeonardi.it • www.limoncello.co.uk
How much? From approx £18/$32/€26
Produced by Giovanni Leonardi, a family business established in 1871, and another quality name to look for.

V&C CONDIMENTO
Where? Valvona & Crolla, 19 Elm Row, Edinburgh EH7, Scotland • 00 44 131 556 6066 • www.valvonacrolla.co.uk
How much? Approximately £11/$20/€15
The Italian deli Valvona & Crolla, founded in 1934 by the Contini family to serve the local immigrant community, is an Edinburgh institution. Their own-brand 'condimento' isn't strictly a balsamic vinegar, but it is one of the best commercial balsamic 'dressings' you will find. Produced in the Emilia Romagna region of Italy, this bargain is a great store-cupboard staple – a little goes a long, long way.

Caviar

Almas Caviar

Where?

Various sources including: The Caviar House & Prunier, 161 Piccadilly, London, W1 • 00 44 207 409 0445 • www.caviarhouse.com

How much?

Approx £920/$1,380/€1,030 for 50g (1 ½oz)

Caviar is currently in a state of contention since the US put a ban on beluga imports. The reason behind this is the massively depleted numbers of beluga sturgeon; the population has fallen by 90 percent in recent years due to overfishing, poaching and pollution. Caviar is the roe – or eggs – from one of 27 species of sturgeon. It is up to just three species to produce most of the world's supply: beluga sturgeon (beluga caviar), Russian sturgeon (osetra caviar) and stellate sturgeon (sevruga caviar).

Almas caviar

The most prized caviar is also the most difficult to obtain. Almas, which is pale – almost white – in colour, comes from very rare albino sturgeons. Almas tastes creamy, smooth and almost buttery, and has an 18-month waiting list at The Caviar House in Piccadilly, where it is sold in a gold tin. In Iran, in fact, this caviar used to be the preserve of the Shah – and anyone else found eating it would have their right hand chopped off.

The delicate nature of caviar means it should never be touched with any metal other than gold. Instead, serve the eggs using a mother-of-pearl spoon, the traditional utensil, although a wooden or plastic one will do; 14–28g (½–1oz) per person should suffice. Caviar is best eaten on blinis with sour cream. Gourmands suggest separating the caviar and sour cream, and eating each alternately on separate blinis to provide a delightful contrast. Wash down with a glass of champagne or a shot of vodka.

'*Almas caviar is my favourite as it makes a great starter. In fact, I used it for the dinner I prepared for President Putin and Tony Blair.*'

Gordon Ramsay, Michelin-star chef

BELUGA

Where? Various sources including: www.imperialcaviar.co.uk

How much? Approx £160/$240/€180 for 50g (1½oz)

Beluga caviar is another fine choice, in other words, the beluga that *isn't* Almas. Again, the taste is creamy and smooth – although not as buttery as the Almas – and the colour is a dark grey.

TSAR NICOULAI, CALIFORNIAN ESTATE OSETRA

Where? www.tsarnicoulai.com

How much? From approx £193/$289/€216 for 50g (1½oz)

When sturgeon were discovered living in Californian rivers, the American caviar industry revved into action. This is an excellent way for Americans to get around the US ban. Osetra have larger eggs than beluga and are brown in colour, with a distinctive nutty taste.

COULD CAVIAR BE THE SECRET TO A FLAWLESS COMPLEXION?

Caviar is one of the most nutritionally complete foods – it contains 47 vitamins and minerals – and is therefore extremely good for you, especially for your skin. Skincare guru Eve Lom (she of muslin cloth fame) has been eating caviar since she was a child.

'What interests me, as a skincare specialist, is to see the effect of caviar on my skin and hair,' she says. 'The oils lubricate my skin and make my hair much glossier. My interest in skin is all about texture, and no cream or cosmetic in the world is as effective as eating 50g (1½ oz) of caviar. It doesn't matter if your skin is naturally dry or oily – the results are truly amazing.'

Prestige Selection caviar from Caviar House

Champagne

Louis Roederer Brut Premier

Where?

www.bbr.com • www.oddbins.com • All good wine merchants

How much?

Approx £35/$50/€40

It would seem that we're all adhering to the famous creed of Lily Bollinger, who hailed from the champagne house of the same name and once said: 'I drink champagne when I'm happy, and I drink it when I'm sad… otherwise I never touch it – unless I'm thirsty.' Champagne consumption is higher now than ever before, especially among women, who are 13 times more likely to crack open the bubbly than men, making it no longer the preserve of special occasions.

So which one should you drink? The vast majority of wine writers rate Louis Roederer as the number one non-vintage champagne – it constantly tops blind tastings and was many an expert's recommendation as the best way to bring in the new millennium. Connoisseurs rave about its tiny, perfectly formed bubbles and clean taste, which has a creamy, buttery finish. Then there's the smell – a mix of toasted brioche and honey (many good champagnes have a distinct biscuity taste), combined with the scent of berries thanks to the profusion of pinot noir grapes – the proportion is roughly two to one pinot noir to chardonnay. Louis Roederer is also aged in wood, which is something of a rarity – most non-vintage champagnes are aged in stainless steel or glass containers – and comes from the same producer as the much more 'bling' Cristal. Unlike the infamous Cristal, however, Brut Premier is classy and infinitely more accessible. The perfect party champagne, in fact.

Louis Roederer Brut Premier

The best way to get your kick from champagne? Serve it at 7°C/45°F (any warmer, and the contents will foam excessively) from a flute glass that will preserve the bubbles. Drink with caviar, oysters or smoked salmon – asparagus also complements the taste extremely well. The very, very best way to enjoy it, though, is on its own.

POL ROGER CUVÉE SIR WINSTON CHURCHILL

Where? Selected merchants such as www.bbr.com

• www.polroger.co.uk

How much? Approx £98/$141/€104

The family-owned champagne house was a favourite of Sir Winston Churchill, who quaffed the bubbles during the dark days of the war, often from a pint glass. 'In defeat I need it, in victory I deserve it,' he once declared. After his death in 1965, they added a black boarder to the labels of bottles sold in the UK, as a tribute to their most famous client. Then, 20 years on, the house launched Cuvée Sir Winston Churchill, a vintage blend in which the Pinot Noir dominates combined with Chardonnay producing a full-bodied result, just the way Sir Winston enjoyed it. In an attempt to uphold its upmarket image, Pol Roger ensures the Cuvée is only sold by merchants who won't then resell bottles to clubs frequented by footballers and their ilk.

Pol Roger Cuvée

KRUG GRAND CUVÉE

Where? www.bbr.com • All good wine merchants
How much? From approx £123/$180/€137

Dating back to 1843, this champagne house offers no entry-level bottles. 'We start where others stop,' they claim. Krug also has a distinctive taste: slightly dusty with hints of dried fruit, toasted brioche, roses and violets, a unique bouquet that is said to be the result of storing champagne in oak barrels.

The typical bottle of champagne contains 49 million bubbles.

Krug Grand Cuvée

Chocolate

Artisan du Chocolat

Where?
89 Lower Sloane Street, London, SW1 • 00 44 207 824 8365 •
www.artisanduchocolat.com

How much?
Tasting Selection Box £25/$38/€28

Artisan du Chocolat

Multi-Michelin-star British chef Gordon Ramsay describes Artisan du Chocolat as 'the Bentley of chocolate' and it is the only range he will serve in his restaurants. Ditto Heston Blumenthal, owner of The Fat Duck, 'The Best Restaurant in the World', according to *Restaurant* magazine for several years running. All of which is praise indeed, especially for such a young company (it has only been running since 1999) – and a British one, at that.

Traditionally, the world's best chocolatiers have been confined to Belgium, Switzerland and France. The ambitious aim of the cofounder, Gerard Coleman, is to make Artisan du Chocolat the best in the world, while ensuring that quality is never, ever compromised; hence the company has no immediate plans for expansion. Indeed, the self-confessed perfectionist is behind the manufacture of every single chocolate and the company, like the ever-innovative Blumenthal, is known for its use of unusual ingredients – flavours include sesame, Bramley apple, green cardamom and tobacco. Banana and thyme is its best-seller, a thin shell of intense chocolate encasing two very different flavours that somehow balance each other magnificently.

Coleman believes that part of his success is down to the British public's enthusiasm to try new things. 'They are more open to experimentation than the French, Belgians or Germans, who have more defined tastes and don't want you to start putting cardamom in their chocolate', he has said. Coleman, himself a chef by training, decided that Britain was missing a top-notch chocolatier. He spent time working with esteemed Belgian chocolate company Pierre Marcolini (*see below*) before branching out on his own. Each of his chocolates is freshly made and, once bought, should be stored at 15°C/59°F and eaten within a fortnight. The company is passionate about the fact that chocolate is fresh food, as opposed to something pumped up with sugar and preservatives in order to extend its shelf-life. Unlike most chocolatiers, who only use one bean, Coleman uses different beans to complement the different flavours of the centres, all of which are made using the finest raw ingredients. As well as taste, Coleman is also obsessed with texture – be it the crunch of a nutty praline or the silky smoothness of a berry filling – believing this to be another crucial factor in the making of perfect chocolate.

PIERRE MARCOLINI

Where? www.marcolini.be

How much? Orange-thyme praline £5/$9/€7 for three

This Belgian chocolatier has been in business since 1990 and is one of the few who still processes all of his own cocoa beans – according to Belgian law, only producers who make their wares from scratch can technically call themselves 'chocolatiers'. He now has shops in London and Tokyo, as well as Brussels. Best-sellers include his praline; the orange–thyme combination is a particular favourite.

BOUTIQUE CHOCOLATIERS: BEST OF THE REST

Paul A Young Fine Chocolates
This nascent chocolatier is already one of Britain's best and the winner of several awards (his sea-salted caramel comes highly recommended). Everything is made by hand on site. A name to watch.
33 Camden Passage, London, N1
00 44 207 424 5750, www.paulayoung.co.uk

Bernachon
Many chocoholics consider Bernachon – Lyon's most famous chocolatier – to be the best in France. All ingredients are the best of the best: vanilla pods from Madagascar; pistachios from Sicily. His cacao-rich truffles have melted many a gastronome's heart.
42 cours Franklin Roosevelt, Lyon, France
00 33 4 78 24 37 98, www.bernachon.com

Michel Chaudin
Chaudin was head chocolatier at La Maison du Chocolat (*see below*) for many years before going solo, and is now rated as one of the world's very best. His 'Les Pavés', tiny cubes of cocoa-dusted ganache, speared from a box with a toothpick, are sublime, as is his artistry: the shop display often includes such intricate creations as a chocolate Faberge egg and Hermès Kelly handbag complete with chocolate pouch.
149, rue de l'Université, Paris, France
00 33 01 47 53 74 40,

Burie
Brussels may have claimed Belgium's foodie crown, but Antwerp comes a close second, not least because of Burie. The fresh handmade chocolates are to-die-for, in particular the walnut and caramel crunch. In keeping with the city's other famous commodity, Burie also does boxes of 'chocolate diamonds' that make lovely gifts.
Stefaniestraat 8, Antwerp, Belgium
00 32 3 237 1242, www.chocolatier-burie.be

Hirsinger
The pretty town of Arbois in the wine-producing Jura region of France hides another gourmet treasure: Edouard Hirsinger's chocolate shop. Must-tastes include chocolate infused with strawberries and balsamic vinegar, and the range specially developed to accompany the region's fine wines.
Place de la Liberté, Arbois, France
00 33 384 660 697, www.chocolat-hirsinger.com

The Chocolate Line
Dominique Persoone is an up-and-coming superstar chocolatier, and his smart shop in Bruges is one of only three chocolatiers in the Michelin Guide. Renowned for his quirky innovations, he produced snuff for a party for the now-drug-free Rolling Stones. More prosaically, he also makes chocolate for Comme Chez Soi, the famous Michelin-starred restaurant in Brussels.
Simon Stevinplein 19, Brugges, Belgium.
00 32 50 34 10 90, www.thechocolateline.be

La Maison du Chocolat

LA MAISON DU CHOCOLAT
Where? 45–46 Piccadilly, London, W1 • 00 44 207 297 8500 • www.lamaisonduchocolat.com
How much? Bacchus truffles from 70p/$1/€1 each
Robert Linxe of the Paris-based La Maison du Chocolat is known in the industry as 'the creator' and the original superstar chocolatier. He is obsessed with ganache, a gooey centre that is made from cream and chocolate, sometimes adding an infusion. The Bacchus truffle with rum-and-raisin filling is his self-confessed favourite; each raisin is 'tailed and flamed' before being impregnated with a rum vapour.

Claret

Château Mouton Rothschild, 1945

Where?

Nickolls & Perks • www.nickollsandperks.co.uk

Wine Bid • www.winebid.com

Fine & Rare Wine • www.frw.co.uk

Berry Bros. & Rudd • www.bbr.com

How much?

Anything upwards of £4,000/$6,000/€4,485 •
Other vintages start at approx £80/$141/€118

Château
Mouton
Rothschild

Did you know that the actual cost of the wine in a £4 ($6) bottle is usually only about 60p ($1)? Proof, if proof were needed, that when it comes to wine, it really does pay to pay more. But how much more? With claret – and vintage claret, at that – the costs can easily go into the thousands. First, a couple of clarifications: claret is a dry red wine from the Bordeaux region, dark in colour with a fruity, liquorice-tinged flavour. It is best when it matures – drinking it young won't always do it justice. A vintage claret refers to a year when the grapes achieved perfect ripeness. Despite claims to the contrary, there have only been three great claret vintages since the Second World War – 1945, 1961 and 1982. Of course, one never knows a truly great vintage until several years down the line, so when it comes to buying claret it is always worth taking risks.

Nowadays, more people than ever are interested in expensive wine, thanks in part to the influential wine critic Robert Parker and his '100-point' system, but also because of the burgeoning economies of China and Russia. Blue-chip chateaux still attract the most interest: think Château Lafite Rothschild, Château Latour or Château d'Yquem, which is famous for holding back some supplies for later sales. All are names worth noting when purchasing claret.

But what's the best? The answer, of course, is totally subjective – one man's Château Latour is another man's Ribena – but the respected wine magazine *Decanter* recently came up with a suggestion: Château Mouton Rothschild, 1945, the one wine their critics claimed everyone should 'drink before they die'.

The magazine described it as 'intense, concentrated, indescribable … without doubt the greatest claret of the 20th century'. Not bad for a château that only officially received 'Première Cru Classe' (the highest classification possible) in 1973. The château lies opposite Lafite and has been growing vines since the 1720s. Mouton Rothschild's *terroir*, or soil, is formed of deep gravel beds with a subsoil consisting of clay and limestone. Their claret is made up of 85 percent cabernet sauvignon, 10 percent cabernet franc and 5 percent merlot. Oenophiles can tour the château, taking in the original artwork by Picasso, but the cellar, which houses 35,000 bottles of untouched wine, some dating back to 1859, is strictly off-limits.

Incidentally, a tip for cheaper claret – and indeed red wine in general – is to decant it into a glass vessel before drinking. This will add oxygen, instantly making the most bog-standard bottle taste like a million dollars. A similar trick can be done with white wine using a ceramic jug to keep it cooler.

Château Cheval Blanc

CHÂTEAU PÉTRUS
Where? Corney & Barrow • www.corneyandbarrow.com
How much? From approx £115/$178/€130 for a 1995 vintage
A Merlot-dominated claret that has risen to prominence, in part because Robert Parker is such a fan.

CHÂTEAU CHEVAL BLANC
Where? Berry Bros. & Rudd • www.bbr.com
How much? From approx £300/$450/€336
A claret that's found fame for a very different reason – it featured in the acclaimed movie *Sideways*. According to Miles, the film's anti-hero, this is 'the only wine worthy of seducing a woman'. It has an unusually high percentage of cabernet franc grapes, which doesn't usually produce good wines on its own, except in the case of Château Cheval Blanc. The result is a lush, velvety texture with a slight truffle and mushroom tinge on the tongue. Unlike most clarets, you can drink this one relatively young – after seven or eight years – but ideally wait until it's around 20 years old. Ignore Miles when it comes to vintage, though; despite his claims to 1961, the ultimate is actually 1947. Parker gave this one 100 out of 100.

SIMON BERRY, OF THE QUEEN'S WINE MERCHANTS, BERRY BROS. & RUDD, CHATS ABOUT CLARET.

What makes claret so great?
Simon Berry (SB): 'It's unique. Cabernet sauvignon is grown throughout the world, but the finest clarets are still the greatest wines in that they are never bettered. You might have to pay anything over £50 ($90) a bottle to get something fantastic – but with tickets to football matches costing that nowadays, it's not a lot for one of life's great luxuries.'

How should the perfect glass of claret taste?
SB: 'Almost indescribable – but with an extraordinary balance of fruit, acidity and density. It will have great complexity – a taste that changes and develops over time – and will linger in the mouth for a significant period. It's instantly recognizable, though, once you've experienced a few.'

What are good, more affordable, options?
SB: 'The 1990s and 1989s are wonderful now. And great properties from 1997 are very affordable.'

For the first-time buyer, what advice would you give?
SB: 'Find a good wine merchant – someone who you trust, and who will take you through what will end up as a journey of discovery. And remember that it's all about personal taste. Really, the only important question is: is it good to drink?'

Coffee

Kopi Luwak

Where?

Edible, 8 The Piper Building, London, SW6 • 00 44 207 691 7341 • Selfridges, 400 Oxford Street, London, W1 • 00 44 800 123 400 • www.selfridges.co.uk • www.tastesoftheworld.net • www.animalcoffee.com

How much?

Approx £175/$260/€195 for a 450g (1lb) bag

A good cup of coffee should be treated in the same manner as a fine wine – sniffed, savoured and respected. The best blend is down to personal taste, but the most expensive – and the most rare – is that ground from the kopi luwak. These beans from Indonesia are produced in the most unusual way: from the excrement of civets who feast on coffee cherries, eating them whole, bean and all. When they have passed through their bodies, the bean remains, albeit covered in a parchment-like layer. The beans are then collected by locals, who remove the shell and sell them on.

The result, thanks to the civet's gastric juices, is a uniquely smooth flavour that many describe as reminiscent of caramel and chocolate without any hint of bitterness. Edible, the bean's main distributor in Britain, says customers include Damian Hirst.

Civet Coffee, Kopi Luwak

JAMAICA BLUE MOUNTAIN

Where? www.tastesoftheworld.net • www.fortnumandmason.com • Reputable delis and food halls worldwide

How much? Approx £37/$55/€40 for a 250g bag

With the exception of the Kopi Luwak, Blue Mountain is the coffee synonymous with high prices. This is because the beans are so hard to reach – they grow 2,100 metres (6,890 feet) above sea-level in Jamaica's Blue Mountains. The result is a sweet, full-bodied cup. Beware of imitations though – there are lots of fakes out there.

UNION HAND-ROASTED

Where? www.unionroasted.com • Waitrose stores nationwide (www.waitrose.com) and www.ocado.com

How much? Approx £3.50/$5/€4 for 227g (8 oz)

Fairtrade coffee now accounts for 4 percent of all coffee sales in the UK, and the best, according to *Ethical Consumer* magazine, is Union Hand-Roasted. Rick Stein and Jamie Oliver probably agree – both chefs serve UHR in their restaurants – although fairtrade coffee is found in precious few other top-end restaurants. The company offers a range of single estate and specially blended coffee.

Ice cream

Corrado Costanzo

Where?

Via Spaventa 7, Noto, Sicily • 00 39 931 835 243

How much?

Prices from £1.20/$1.95/€1.40 a scoop

Anyone with a sweet tooth should get the next flight to Sicily – an island where they even eat ice cream for breakfast, usually in the form of a hollowed-out brioche filled with *gelato* (Italian ice cream). Ice cream was invented here some time around the 8th century, when Arabs inhabiting the island first thought to scoop the ice from the slopes of Mount Etna, and combine it with sugar, milk and flavourings from local products, such as oranges, lemons, almonds and roses. The ideal way, they figured, to stave off the fierce summer heat.

Gelato

The best *gelato* comes from the baroque town of Noto in the south of the island. Here you'll find the world's most mouthwatering scoops at Corrado Costanzo, a *gelateria* that has been running for almost 50 years. Along with the more traditional flavours like vanilla, chocolate and coffee, are more unusual concoctions made from mulberry, rose and jasmine. Like the Arabs, Costanzo is fastidious about preparing his puddings with the very best local ingredients, only using flowers picked in the evening, for instance, when they are at their most fragrant.

The bestseller is *granita al mandarino*, a sorbet made with the juiciest local mandarin oranges; the result is the epitome of refreshing zinginess, and not in the least bit tart. People will travel for miles – continents, even – simply to sample what Costanzo calls 'the taste of Sicily in your mouth'. Of course this is not strictly an ice cream – but then neither is *gelato*; unlike most ice cream found in Britain and the US, *gelato* is made using milk, not cream.

GREEN & BLACK'S ORGANIC ICE CREAM

Where? Good delis and supermarkets such as Waitrose and Ocado • www.greenandblacks.com

How much? £3.90/$5.70/€4.19 for a 500ml tub

This ice cream is as good as you would expect from a company that has many, many fans. Made with fresh cream, and in four flavours, the vanilla uses actual vanilla (a surprising number of ice cream companies don't) and the chocolate, a particular stand-out, contains lashings and lashings of the company's famously delicious dark chocolate. As well as being organic, all ingredients are ethically sourced.

ALBA GOLD

Where? 72 High Street, London, W3 • 00 44 208 992 5748 • Selected restaurants and delis nationwide, such as Trinity Stores in Balham in London (www.trinitystores.co.uk) and Tavola, 155 Westbourne Grove, London, W11

How much? £4/$6/€4.50 for 500ml (17 fl oz)

Alba Gold, a proper Italian artisan ice cream, is only available in small quantities since most is sold directly on to Michelin-starred restaurants. The company's ingredients are the finest available: pistachios from Sicily, for instance, or sun-matured strawberries from Morocco. The tiramisu flavour is exceptional.

THE GLOBETROTTING GELATO-ITE

Wherever you are in the world, it's good to know that a decent scoop of vanilla is close at hand. Below is a guide for the globetrotting gelato-ite:

Giolitti
After Sicily, Rome is the best place in Italy to find ice cream. This atmospheric café has been going since 1900 and serves some of the most heavenly scoops around.
Via Uffici del Vicario 40, Rome, Italy
00 39 06 699 1243

Gelatauro
Since Bologna is the gastronomic heart of Italy, the locals are extremely fussy when it comes to their treats. The locals decree this place the best for mind-blowing ice cream.
Via San Vitale 90, Bologna, Italy
00 39 051 230 049

Persicco
Due to its Italian heritage, Argentine *helado* is some of the best in the world. Persicco is the leading up-market chain, thanks to its all-natural ingredients.
Migueletes 886, Palermo, Buenos Aires, Argentina, plus branches
00 54 11 57 78 55 00

Berthillon
If too many patisserie delicacies are weighing you down, this is widely regarded as the best ice cream in France.
31 Rue St-Louis-en-L'Ile, Paris, France
00 33 1 43 54 31 61

Morelli's in Harrods
This outpost of the Broadstairs branch offers a bespoke ice cream service in Harrods' famous food hall. The helpful staff will always try to accommodate all tastes – requested flavours have included 'baked beans on toast' and 'pickled onions.'
87-135 Brompton Road, London, SW1
00 44 207 730 1234

Marine Ices
Visiting Italians say this established North London ice cream parlor is the closest thing to being in Rome. Try the lemon sorbet – a particular favourite.
8 Haverstock Hill, London, NW3
00 44 207 482 9003

Serendipity
This Manhattan restaurant, once frequented by Andy Warhol, Jackie Kennedy and Marilyn Monroe, has only one pudding worth ordering: the 'Bipolar' Frrrozen Hot Chocolate.
225 East 60th Street, New York, NY
001 212 838 3531

Coppelia Calle
Havana's infamous ice cream parlor was built as the Revolution's 'gift to the people'. Tourists are guided to a separate outdoor kiosk, but should sneak a look at the futuristic interior of the main 1966 building. In true Socialist style, choices are limited to vanilla, chocolate and caramel.
23 between Calle L and the Malecon, Havana, Cuba

Manni Per Me

Olive oil

Manni Per Me and Per Mio Figlio

Where?

www.manni.biz • 00 39 06 9727 4787

How much?

Approx £19/$29/€22 for 100ml (3½ fl oz)

There's everyday olive oil – the kind you use for cooking – and then there's the special stuff, the gourmet liquid gold reserved for drizzling, dipping and savouring. Manni Per Me is one of the world's most expensive olive oils, but, for once, the eyebrow-raising prices are in sync with quality, as this is also the world's very best.

The oil was created in 2000, when Italian filmmaker Armando Manni became a father for the first time and wanted to find the purest olive oil possible for his son. For this he needed science and enlisted the help of the University of Florence. Boffins there pinpointed the exact time the olives should be picked for them to be at their richest in antioxidants and have the fullest flavour. Manni bought some groves on Mount Amiata in southern Tuscany and put the research into practice.

The result of all this careful planning is two oils. *Per Mio Figlio* (for my child) is ideal for babies and young children – Madonna uses it for Rocco and Lourdes – and has a smooth, buttery taste. *Per Me* (for me) is for adults and has a full-flavoured and peppery taste. It's so rich, in fact, that enthusiasts claim you can use 50 percent less oil than you normally would – which is one way to save money. The difference in taste between the two oils is because olives from higher up the mountain are used for *Per Me* as these have a more intense flavour. Production is limited to 2,500 litres (550 gallons) a year. The oil can only be purchased over the internet and is sent out in specially temperature-controlled containers by overnight courier.

Giorgio Locatelli, of upscale pasta haven Locanda Locatelli in London, apparently went nuts upon his first tasting of Per Me, instantly ordering a huge batch for use in his restaurant. It is also used in Pierre Gagnaire in Paris, in Per Se in New York, in The Fat Duck in Bray, and in The French Laundry in Napa Valley.

Chefs shout Manni's praise from the roofs of their Michelin-starred restaurants. 'It's a rare breed of person who strives for perfection in his chosen line of work', says Thomas Keller of the French Laundry. 'Armando Manni personifies this determination – he has successfully produced the best and healthiest extra virgin olive oil on the market.'

'When I first tasted Manni's oils, I knew I had tasted something amazing.'

Jean-Georges Vongerichten of Jean-Georges in New York

NÚÑEZ DE PRADO

Where? Good supermarkets and delis, such as www.deandeluca.com • www.zabars.com • www.papedeli.co.uk
• for stockists, see www.nunezdepradousa.com
How much? Approx £17/$25/€18 for one litre

Spain is the biggest producer of olive oil in the world – it has around 370 million olive trees – and certain olive oil aficionados prefer the fruitier Spanish oils to the Italian varieties. Núñez de Prado, produced organically in Andalusia since 1795, is one of the best, praised for its sublime taste, a combination of fresh grass, almonds and butter.

NICOLAS ALZIARI

Where? 14 Rue St-François-de-Paule, 06300, Nice, France • www.alziari.com.fr • 00 33 4 93 85 76 92 • Good delis such as Harvey Nichols
How much? Approx £11.50/$17.50/€13.00 for 500ml (17 fl oz)

Few visitors leave Nice without buying this oil in its distinctive blue and yellow tin. Alziari uses small black olives crushed on a millstone that was powered by the neighbouring river until relatively recently. The resulting taste is gorgeously buttery. Use this to make the perfect salade niçoise.

Nicolas Alziari

A BRIEF GLOSSARY OF OLIVE OIL TERMS

Understanding the wording on a bottle of olive oil is a little like deciphering a bottle of wine – although it should be noted that, unlike wine, olive oil does not improve with age; instead it has a shelf life of about a year. The best are sold in coloured glass bottles, as light and heat can be harmful to the oil. Greener olive oils are made using olives earlier in the season – because they're not as juicy as when they are ripe, this type uses up more olives and is therefore more expensive.

• **Single estate**: From a single family business or farm. Two of the best in Tuscany are Capezzana and Badia a Coltibuono.
• **Blended**: An oil made using olives from different estates, varieties, regions, sometimes even countries.
• **First cold press**: Oil from the first pressing of the olives, with no applied heat.
• **Extra virgin olive oil**: Production is by hand or machine and no chemicals are used. This will have no more than one percent acidity resulting in a fantastic aroma and flavour.
• **Virgin olive oil**: As above, but with an acidity of up to two percent.
• **Olive oil**: Has up to 3.3 percent acidity. This is a lower quality since it's a blend of virgin olive oil and refined (oil that has been chemically treated to neutralize strong tastes). The most common olive oil.
• **Unfiltered**: Contains small bits of olive; will have lots of flavour but sediment at the bottom.

Spice

MM Spices

Where?
M/S Mahesh Kumar Mohan Das, Shop
No 206/3, Clock Tower, Jodhpur, India
How much?
From £1/$1.50/€1.20

MM Spices

India is the motherland of spice – venture into any market and you can smell the spice-sellers selling sachets from hessian sacks a mile off. The only problem is the bewildering array before you, coupled with merchants understandably unused to dealing with curious foreigners.

Which is where MM Spices comes in. The Jodhpur shop, close to the main square, is both accessible and fun. It even has celebrity endorsement – the actor Jeremy Irons often visits Jodhpur for antiques, the other ware for which the city is famous, and will pop here for some seasoning. Plus the proprietor, King Rose, is one shopkeeper you won't forget in a hurry. This self-styled Bollywood hero, complete with medallion, moustache and a pair of jeans that leaves nothing to the imagination, is the ultimate salesman. The result? It's virtually impossible to leave empty-handed.

Luckily, this is one of the best spice shops in India and sells its stock to restaurants nationwide. King Rose sits customers down on a plastic stool and propels them into sensory overload, encouraging them to smell, taste and touch his entire stock, from powdered turmeric, saffron, cinnamon bark and a million varieties of tea, to the 'winter tonic', a sort of natural viagra for men.

Amateur cooks can pick up bags of masala, a blend of different spices, for about 250 rupees (£3/$6/€4), including an easy recipe for making the most out-of-this-world curry. All this *and* a drawstring silk bag to carry home your wares.

HERBORISTERIE AVENZOAR
Where? 78 Bis Derb N'Khel, Rahba Lakdima, Marrakech, Morocco
How much? From £1/$1.50/€1.20
The world's other great spice centre is Morocco. In Marrakech, ask your guide to direct you to Herboristerie Avenzoar for good-quality spices, as well as massages using different plant oils.

THE SPICE SHOP
Where? 1 Blenheim Crescent, London, W11 • 00 44 207 221 4448 • www.thespiceshop.co.uk
How much? From £1/$1.50/€1.20
This tiny Notting Hill shop has the best all-round selection of spices in Britain, including unusual choices such as jade seaweed salt and four types of cumin. The owner travels the world sourcing the very best spices, while gaining a specialist knowledge that's second to none. The shop also has an excellent mail order service.

Tea

Silver Needles

Where?

Various specialist teashops and tea websites, including:
www.theteatable.com and www.greysteas.co.uk •
Claridge's tearoom, Brook Street, London, W1 •
00 44 207 629 8860

How much?

£18/$27/€20 per 125g (4½oz)

Of all liquids consumed by the world's population, 40 percent is tea. And whether black or green, it all comes from the same source – the leaves of the shrub *camellia sinensis*. Variations are down to the treatment: black tea is fermented, green is steamed and dried and oolong is partially fermented – the oxidation process is stopped before it is complete.

The British are probably best known for their love of tea, especially given their mindset – that a cup of tea and sympathy can solve just about any problem. Tea first came to Britain in 1644, thanks to the East India Company, and by the 18th century it had become the country's most popular beverage. So much so that following the Boston Tea Party, patriotic Americans showed their allegiance to their country by swapping tea-drinking for coffee.

For a really special brew, connoisseurs should try Silver Needles, one of the rarest teas – and therefore one of the most expensive. It is also a white tea, a type that has become increasingly popular in recent years due to the fact that it is packed full of antioxidants – up to three times more than green, in fact.

White tea is made from immature tea leaves that must be picked before the buds are fully opened. Silver Needles comes from the Fujian Province of China and is picked within a two-day period in early spring. The tea gets its name from the dried leaves, which are needle-shaped and silver in colour due to the fuzz that still covers the bud. The result is a tea admired for its full-bodied and exceptionally delicate flavour.

Once the preserve of the Chinese Emperor and *nobody* else – 900 years ago, during the Song Dynasty, a cup of this tea would have cost you your head – it is now readily available over the internet.

FORTNUM & MASON

Where? 181 Piccadilly, London, W1 • 00 44 207 734 8040 • www.fortnumandmason.com

How much? From £7/$10/€8 for a 250g (8 oz) tin

The upmarket grocer has a rare tea bar that sells one of the best selections of uncommon teas in the world. Popular varieties include rose pouchong, Russian caravan and Margaret's Hope.

MARIAGE FRÈRES

Where? 30 Rue du Bourg-Tibourg, 75004, Paris, France • 00 33 1 43 47 1854 • www.mariagefreres.com

How much? £107/$160/€120 per 100g (3½oz)

Another excellent purveyor of tea is Mariage Frères, a Parisian company that sells over 50 types of Darjeeling. Brumes d'Himalaya ('Himalayan mists') is their most expensive; the leaf tips are picked from the 'first flush' (in other words, the first spring harvest) at a single estate in Darjeeling. Incidentally, most 'Darjeeling' sold in shops is nothing of the kind, since it comes from Kenya or Sri Lanka. Beware of imitations.

Vodka

Jean-Marc XO

Jean-Marc
XO

Where?
www.jmxo.com • All good food-halls and off-licences
How much?
£40/$60/€45 for a standard bottle

Russian, Swedish, Polish – which vodka is the best? French, actually. Jean-Marc XO has none of the vodka 'afterburn' (the feeling as the liquid travels down the throat) that's so familiar with many Eastern European brands. This is because it is made in the same manner as cognac (hence the 'XO'). Indeed, the brand recently won a prestigious taste test when the US Beverage Tasting Institute rated it the best vodka ever, with a score of 96 out of 100.

The company was started by Jean-Marc Daucourt, a French distiller from Cognac. 'Vodka isn't big in France,' he explains, 'but I discovered it 20 years ago when I lived in America, and knew that we could do better.'

Produced with the same copper stills that are used in the cognac-making process, the vodka is distilled nine times to remove all the impurities – most vodkas are distilled twice at the most – then micro-oxygenated to further kill the afterburn. Jean-Marc Daucourt is the only company in the world that does this. The result is the perfect vodka – clear, with floral notes, anise and a pleasingly powdery feel in the mouth. Best of all, it doesn't taste too alcoholic – it's as odourless and as flavourless as it gets, the way vodka ought to be. In fact, you can merrily drink Jean-Marc XO on the rocks without wincing.

GREY GOOSE

Where? All good off-licences
How much? £30/$45/€34

The world's most popular super-premium brand is also blended and bottled in Cognac. The making of the company was winning a taste test in 1998 – the same one Jean-Marc XO pipped them to more recently. A favourite with many top mixologists, Grey Goose has a creamy taste and is widely available.

BELVEDERE

Where? All good off-licences
How much? £26/$39/€29

Another popular super-premium brand, Belvedere is made in Poland from rye (most Polish vodka comes from potatoes). The taste is creamy with hints of vanilla, and is the bling vodka choice – Belvedere is the long-standing favourite with the hip-hop community.

Beauty

'The best thing is to look natural,
but it takes a lot of makeup
to look natural.'

Calvin Klein,
fashion designer,
1942—

Aftershave

Creed Green Irish Tweed

Where?
38 Avenue Pierre 1er de Serbie, 75008, Paris, France • 00 33 1 47 20 58 02 •
www.creedfragrances.co.uk

How much?
Approx £86/$129/€97

Green Irish Tweed is Creed's bestselling fragrance for gentlemen. The aftershave was originally created for none other than Cary Grant, surely the original chap. Wearers today are just as suave: George Clooney, Pierce Brosnan, Robbie Williams, David Beckham – even Prince Charles is a fan.

Part of Green Irish Tweed's charm is the way it manages to smell so light – there's no overpowering afterburn here. The balanced blend of floral, green and woody notes include verbena, violet leaves, Florentine iris, sandalwood and ambergris. It could be said that Creed started the current trend for bespoke scents, as all but two of their fragrances were originally made exclusively for their wearers. Spring Flowers, for instance, was created for Audrey Hepburn, while Madonna has spent thousands and waited three years for Creed to make her own couture scent, a process that is based on the wearer's personality, passions and olfactory preferences.

Creed, established in 1760, is one of only a handful of perfume houses still privately owned. The current owner, Oliver Creed, is something of a scent obsessive, sourcing the purest essence of rose from Bulgaria and Morocco, jasmine and irises from Italy, tuberose from India and genuine Parma violets. The most expensive of these is the Bulgarian rose, which costs between £28,000 and £44,000 per kilo ($50,000 to $80,000 for 2lbs), more than 30 times the price of beluga caviar.

Creed Green Irish Tweed

Creed still makes all of its perfumes using the traditional infusion technique. The components are weighed, mixed and filtered by hand, then left to seep for weeks, while Oliver tinkers to make each batch perfect. The oils used are always slightly different, which means that the scents vary in fragrance year on year, rather like a fine wine. Experts claim you can instantly distinguish a Creed fragrance, as their scents are notably deeper, richer and more eccentric than any others. In fact, many Creed scents are initially rejected by department store buyers for smelling too unusual. To appreciate Creed, it would seem, takes time, as most of the rejected fragrances end up bestsellers. Creed also takes a deep pocket – developing a passion for their fragrances is an expensive habit, but, given the company of their wearers, it is well worth it.

Parfums de Nicolai New York

PARFUMS DE NICOLAI NEW YORK

Where? 101a Fulham Road, London, SW3 • 00 44 207 581 0922
• www.pnicolai.com
How much? £20/$30/€23
Made by Patricia de Nicolai, the granddaughter of Pierre Guerlain, the esteemed nose Dr Luca Turin describes this, one of his favourite aftershaves, as 'more a companion for life than a mere perfume, a hugely complex and exquisitely balanced citrus-warm composition that never shouts but glows mysteriously at close range'. Indeed the spicy scent, the ingredients of which include bergamot, cloves, amber and vetiver, is highly coveted by knowledgeable cologne-lovers. Quite an achievement given that Parfums de Nicolai receives scant publicity.

CHRISTIAN DIOR EAU SAVAGE

Where? All good perfume shops and department stores
How much? Prices from £22/$33/€25
Famous for its archetypal 'aftershavey' smell – described by some as 'the very essence of a man' – this was actually the first mass-marketed scent also used by women. Eau Savage was created in 1966, and is still the best-selling fragrance in France.

What every gentleman should have in his bathroom cabinet

In the first instance a gentleman should think English. D. R. Harris & Co. (www.drharris.co.uk) of St James's is widely regarded as having the best shaving soap – opt for almond – while Geo. F. Trumper (www.trumpers.com), the Mayfair barbers founded in 1875, has what must be one of the largest selections of razors in the world. For a steady shave try the Warwick, an Edwardian-style razor available with a Gillette Mach-3 blade fitting, which is the best blade.

For the perfect shaving brush, what about one made of pure silver-tip badger from brush experts Kent (www.kentbrushes.com)? Alternatively, try Czech & Speake (www.czechspeake.com), or Truefitt & Hill (www.truefitt-tandhill.com). The ultimate shaving oil, which is much more efficient than foam or gel, isn't quite so exclusive. King of Shaves is recommended by all the best barbers, even the most traditional, and is available at all good pharmacies.

Bath oil

Aromatherapy Associates Deep Relax

Where?

Leading spas worldwide • Space NK • mail order OO
44 8569 7030 • www.aromatherapyassociates.com

How much?

£29.95/$42/€32.20

So much more indulgent than plain old bubble bath, a quality bath oil is the ultimate tool in relaxation. It should delight the olfactory senses, transform your bathroom into a fragrant mini-spa and leave your skin coated in a light silky film. Aromatherapy Associates' award-winning Deep Relax Bath & Shower oil is the most effective we've come across. Its soothing ingredients, including camomile, sandalwood and vertivert, along with a luxurious shot of coconut oil, are the perfect antidote to today's stressed-out lifestyle.

SHU UEMURA PLEASURE OF JAPANESE BATH

Where? Selected department stores and Shu Uemura stores worldwide • www.shuuemura.co.jp • www.shuuemura-usa.com

How much? £19.57/$40/€21

When Karl Lagerfeld takes a bath, there's only one bath oil that will do: Shu Uemura's Pleasure of Japanese Bath. In fact, the Paris-based designer admits to using a whole bottle per bath. Launched over a decade ago, the product was taken off the market in 2000 but public outcry – and protest from Lagerfeld himself – ensured its speedy return. Available in four fragrant options, it's Yuzu, a zesty Japanese citron scent, that sets our olfactory senses on fire.

NEOM LUXURY ORGANICS BATH OIL

*Neom Luxury
Organics bath oil*

Where? www.neomorganics.com

How much? £32/$45/€34.40

This divine bath oil made with 70 percent organic ingredients and 30 percent pure essential oils, is so potent you only need a teeny capful to transform your bathroom into a heady zen-zone. Its Complete Bliss blend evokes feelings of calm thanks to its high concentration of Moroccan rose.

BLISSFUL BODY OILS

Body oils are fast becoming an essential part of the beauty regime. Three brilliant oils we rate above competitors are:

Ligne St Barth's Avocado oil

Favoured by Kate Moss and friends, this can be used all over the body and even in the hair.
www.lignestbarth.com

Jurlique's Rose Body oil

A subtly fragrant organic oil, which is a fantastic and gentle moisturiser for the body.
www.jurlique.com

Mama Mio O Mega Body Oil

Great for preventing stretch marks during pregnancy.
www.mamamio.com

Blusher

Sisley's Phyto-blush Éclat

Where?
Selected department stores worldwide •
www.sisley-cosmetics.co.uk •
www.cosmeticamerica.com

How much?
£39.50/$58.85/€42.47

Blusher has been used for centuries to enhance natural glow and healthiness. After a flurry of cream and liquid varieties, classic powder blusher has made a comeback. One of the best we've ever tried is Sisley's Phyto-blush Éclat. The French skincare and cosmetic company, established in 1976 by Hubert d'Ornano, was pioneering the use of plants and aromatherapy in cosmetics long before it was fashionable. Shade 4 'Pinky Rose' is a classic rosy pink presented in a slim rectangular mirror compact with a swish slimline brush for effortless application. The brand's more recently launched Phyto-Touches Peach-Gold duo is a powder compact designed for paler complexions, creating a gorgeous, dewy glow with just a hint of irridescence.

Sisley Phyto-blush Éclat

Ruby & Millie Cheek Color

RUBY & MILLIE CHEEK COLOR
Where? www.boots.com
How much? £12.50/$17.71/€13.44
Neither too orange nor too pink, this best-selling blusher is favoured for its fine texture and ability to suit most skin tones. The brand's more recently launched glide-on Face Gloss arrives in a neat transparent dispenser and can be used on cheeks, eyes and lips for an instant pep-me-up.

Chanel Joues Contraste Powder Blush

CHANEL JOUES CONTRASTE POWDER BLUSH
Where? Departments stores nationwide •
www.chanel.com
How much? £27.50/$39/€29.59
Elegantly presented in that classic black square Chanel packaging, this blusher is a make-up bag essential. The perfect size and shape with an effective little blusher brush, the Tea Rose shade ensures English rose prettiness.

Bronzer

St Tropez Self Tan Bronzing Mousse

St Tropez
Self Tan
Bronzing
Mousse

Where?

www.sttropeztan.com • For stockists call 00 44 115 983 6363

How much?

£19/$38/€29

Despite the fact that we're all more wary of sun-exposure than ever before, due to side effects that range from ageing of the skin to melanoma, the desire for a tan refuses to fade. In fact, looking lean and bronzed – but not tangerine – is still highly desirable. It is best to go to a salon and have fake tan applied by a professional, but if you're short on time and cash, and prepared to do it yourself, the best product you can use is St Tropez's Self Tan Bronzing Mousse. This recent innovation comes from the originators of the first truly realistic fake tan, and is a consistent favourite with beauty editors thanks to its velvety, easy-to-apply texture and long-lasting colour. Most importantly, it creates a natural-looking, non-streaky tan.

Clarins Self
Tanning
Instant Gel

CLARINS SELF TANNING INSTANT GEL

Where? Department stores worldwide

How much? £15.17/$32/€22.34

A light transparent gel that's easy to apply – it glides quickly and fluidly over the body and develops into a natural healthy tan within a couple of hours.

LANCÔME FLASH BRONZER AIRBRUSH

Where? www.lancome.com • Department stores worldwide

How much? £20.50/$28/€27.75

This spray bronzer, raved about by Jessica Simpson and Kylie Minogue, is extremely easy to use: just angle it a few inches from the body and spray away. The very fine mist coats every millimetre of skin and is absorbed easily. Best of all, a natural colour will develop within a couple of hours.

BRILLIANT BRONZERS FOR THE FACE

There's a difference between bronzers for the body and those for the face: the latter should be more sensitive and moisturizing. The best of them all is Sisley's Self Tanning Gel (www.sisley-cosmetics.co.uk), which develops a natural tan within a couple of hours of being applied (available at Harrods in London and Bergdorf Goodman in New York); while Helena Rubenstein's glitter-tinged Golden Beauty Sun Tan Express gel comes in a close second (www.helenarubinstein.com). We also rate Lancome's Flash Bronzer with vitamin E for sheer ease and value for money (www.lancome.com), and Fake Bake's 'The Face', which includes peptides to help prevent those pesky wrinkles (www.fakebake.co.uk).

Compact

Givenchy Prisme

Where?
www.givenchy.com • Department stores worldwide
How much?
From £25/$38/€28

Givenchy Prisme

One of the most practical, pretty and glamorous make-up items a girl can have, a good compact is a handbag necessity and a quality mirrored style is a must.

Founded by Hubert de Givenchy in 1957, Parfums Givenchy was an instant hit, becoming one of the most desirable beauty brands in the world thanks, no doubt, to the brand's associations with the screen icon of the day, Audrey Hepburn. The French company has maintained its elegant image with exquisite offerings, such as the Prisme pressed powder quartet, which allows the user to blend together a perfect shade to match the required skin tone. Available in nine different shades from a pretty pastel white to 'Impertinent Rose' and 'Cool Beige', its angular, black-lacquer packaging makes it one of the most beautifully designed compacts around.

Chantecaille

CHANTECAILLE
Where? www.chantecaille.com • Department stores worldwide
How much? £42/$63/€47
French-born, US-based Sylvie Chanticaille, the former force behind Prescriptives, has created some of the best foundations and powders in the world. Her finely textured compact make-up powder foundation, presented in a galvanized nickel container, is one of the best compacts on the market. The pale shades are particularly good and an excellent option for those with fairer skins. Available in eight shades, including shell, camel and peach.

SHU UEMURA
Where? 24 Neal Street, London, WC2 • 00 44 207 240 7635 •
www.shuuemura.com • Department stores worldwide
How much? £23/$35/€26
A light powder designed to feel as soft as loose powder, with reflective flecks that can eliminate shine in one dusting. We also love the simple, streamlined Japanese-style packaging: a chic addition to any handbag.

Shu Uemura

And the best loose powder ...

With a delicate gold shimmer, **T. Le Clerc's classic Banane Powder** is the legendary loose powder. It was first created in 1881 and is a fine, soft powder that achieves an instant matt finish once applied over foundation. Make-up artists adore the stuff, as does a host of celebrities, including Madonna, Jennifer Aniston and Drew Barrymore.

Face cream

Arcona Magic White Ice

Where?
www.glowgetter.co.uk • www.drugstore.com

How much?
£29/$38/€31.20

Arcona Magic White Ice

It's a million-dollar question in a billion-dollar industry – what is the best face cream in the world? Skins vary as much as body shape, hair texture and colouring. There are thousands of creams, ranging from ultra-cheap (*see facing page*) to expensive and exclusive emollients to cater for this huge market, so pinpointing just one is practically impossible. According to recent scientific research, venix, the gunky white stuff that covers newborn babies, is apparently the best moisturizer in the world. Eeew. And yes, scientists are working out how they can recreate this and sell it in a jar. But in the meantime, we'll have to make do with good old-fashioned cream moisturizers, and if we had to pick the best, it would be Arcona's Magic White Ice Hydrate AM/PM. Arcona is a Los Angeles beauty brand that pioneers the use of cosmeceutical-grade ingredients such as enzymes, antioxidants and amino acids while keeping products free of harmful parabens, petrochemicals, perfumes and dyes.

This brand is all about results and its moisturiser really does leave the skin feeling softer and looking more dewy after just a few days' use. An affordable, light-textured moisturiser that glides on to the skin easily and is absorbed in an instant, this is something of a wonder product.

Natura Bissé Diamond Cream

NATURA BISSÉ DIAMOND CREAM

Where? www.naturabisse.es • Selected department stores worldwide

How much? £170/$265/€170

The silver jar looks expensive and appeals to the inner J-Lo in us all, but it's the cream inside that's valuable. Just one application and you know this is special as it sinks deeply into the skin. OK, so it doesn't contain actual diamonds: instead, the potent ingredients are straight from the sea. It is also packed with grapeseed extract, beta-glucans (derived from dried yeast extract), vitamins C and E, and an oligo-collagen complex. Skin is left feeling buffed and polished.

Elemis Pro-Collagen Marine Cream

ELEMIS PRO-COLLAGEN MARINE CREAM

Where? www.elemis.com • Selected salons and department stores worldwide

How much? £75/$124/€110

Crème de La Mer may be the most expensive marine-based face cream in the world – the newest addition, 'Project Precious', contains the rarest ingredients and costs upwards of £1,000 – but the beautifully light Pro-Collagen Marine Cream from Elemis is a much more versatile and affordable marine-derived option.

It is also easier to apply and suits more skin types. Containing the unique *Padina pavonica* algae (a fan-shaped brown algae hand-picked by scuba divers from the temperate waters off Malta), there is also a helping of porphyridium seaweed, chlorella seaweed, mimosa, rose, and gingko biloba. The best way to experience this cream? Have the Elemis Pro-Collagen Japanese Silk Booster Facial, one of the best facials in the world, at an Elemis spa.

Best bargain moisturizers

- **Pond's face cream** (found at most chemists). Originally invented in 1846 as a medicine by scientist Theron T. Pond who discovered it could heal small wounds, this cream became one of the best selling cosmetic creams of the 20th century and many women, young and old, still swear by it.
- **The Body Shop's Vitamin E Moisture Cream** (www.bodyshop.co.uk). The Body Shop's best-selling product is produced solely from plants and includes antioxidants that protect the skin from the elements. At around £7 ($12), it is also brilliantly affordable.
- **Olay Complete All Day Moisture Lotion** (www.olay.com). A classic fluid moisturizer, now with SPF15, this absorbs into the skin easily. Great for normal skin types.
- **Nivea Creme** (www.nivea.com). Classic Nivea Creme, in its iconic royal blue and white packaging, is the ultimate multifunctional moisturizer as it can be used on the face, body and hands. Good for very dry skins.
- **Weleda Skin Food** (www.weleda.com). A skin-saving natural moisturizer, rich in lanolin and essential oils including lavender and sweet orange, which soothe and nourish very dry skin. Can be used on body and face.

Three of the best organic moisturizers

- **Dr Hauschka's Quince Day Cream** (www.drhauschka.co.uk) is a hit with Kate Moss and Sadie Frost. A lightweight, natural cream, it contains quince and beeswax extracts; both have protective qualities.
- **Jurlique Recover Gel** is a light, vitamin-rich gel that delivers instant refreshing moisturization in one easy application (www.jurlique.com).
- **Barefoot Botanicals Rose Fina Intensive Facial Radiance Cream** (www.barefoot-botanicals.com). An easily absorbed moisturizer packed full of herbal essences.

Facial cleanser

Liz Earle Cleanse & Polish Hot Cloth Cleanser

Where?
www.uk.lizearle.com • dedicated Liz Earle stores, 38-39 Duke of York Square, Kings Road, London, SW3 • 00 44 207 730 9191 • Union, 22 Union Street, Ryde, Isle of Wight • 00 44 1983 813 980 • selected John Lewis stores

How much?
£12.50/$18/€13 for 100ml pump and two muslin cloths

Once a beauty industry insider secret until the word spread; now Liz Earle's bestselling cleanser is multi-award-winning. Suitable for all skin types, its success is largely down to the linen-cloth ritual that accompanies the product (Eve Lom's cult cleaning system is arguably more famous for popularizing this method but we prefer Earle's product for being both lighter and considerably cheaper). First the cleanser is massaged over the skin (facial massage should be a part of any good skincare routine since it stimulates the bloodstream leaving skin glowing). The cloth is then rinsed in hot water and used to 'polish' off the cleanser, a process that also exfoliates the skin; the coup de grace, a splash of cold water. All of which leaves a peachy-clean complexion.

The cleanser – which contains chamomile, rosemary and eucalyptus oil – was first developed 15 years ago by Earle, a beauty journalist whose personal obsession with natural skincare and essential oils transformed her into a businesswoman. Such is Cleanse & Polish's appeal that there is now a 'special' version for men (in a more masculine grey packaging). Earle has even had fan mail from teenage boys – and you know how ungrateful they often are – thanking her for transforming their adolescent complexions.

DERMALOGICA SPECIAL CLEANSING GEL
Where? Stockists nationwide • www.dermalogica.co.uk • 00 44 800 591 818
How much? £17/$24/€18 for 250ml
We've heard so many tales of those with oily or combination skin – coupled with the inevitable pimples – using Dermalogica's cleansing gel and raving about it. This really does work and it clears the skin of impurities. The cleanser is soap-free, so it doesn't dry the skin, and contains a blend of *Quillaja saponaria* (soap bark tree), balm mint and lavender. Once you start using the gel, its fans promise, you won't be able to stop.

SHU UEMURA CLEANSING BEAUTY OIL
Where? Department stores such as Liberty and Harvey Nichols • branches of Space NK and Sephora • For a list of stockists see www.shuuemura-usa.com
How much? £22/$32/€24 for 150ml
One bottle of Shu Uemura's cleansing oil is sold every 30 seconds in Japan, and if you've seen how seriously Japanese women treat their skin (read: *very* seriously) then you'll be itching to try this. Containing green tea extract, renowned for its anti-aging properties, the oil is perfect for dry and sensitive skins. Warm water is added to give the oil a milky quality that is then massaged into the skin before being washed off. It can even remove waterproof mascara, a feat in itself.

Hairbrush

Mason Pearson

Where?
www.masonpearson.com • All
good pharmacies

How much?
Large hairbrush with pure bristle
approx £74/$110/€83

The Mason Pearson hairbrush is a classic and still the best – a bona fide status symbol for the bathroom. Diana, Princess of Wales, always carried a pocket nylon bristle model in her bag, while top hairdressers the world over – think the kind whose names also grace shampoo bottles – recommend this brand to their clientele. Like many great designs, a Mason Pearson brush is all about the details. Part of the reason the brushes work so well is due to a clever pneumatic rubber cushion, which allows the brush to follow the contours of the head and effectively massage the scalp. Mason Pearson, an engineer from Yorkshire, invented the cushion at the height of the Industrial Revolution while working for the British Steam Brush Works. He also invented the handle, specially designed for comfort and originally made of wood. The original style is still available today, although most are now made from plastic that has been carefully hand-polished to remove any sharpened edges.

Brushes come in four sizes: the 'popular large', with six rings of tufts, is suitable for most hair – as a rule of thumb, the longer the hair, the bigger the brush needed. Different hair types require different types of tuft, and Mason Pearson offers three options: natural boar bristle, best for fine to normal hair and less likely to snag the hair than nylon; a mix of nylon and bristle for medium to thick hair and pure nylon – Mason Pearson have developed their own special type of nylon – recommended for very thick hair that tangles. For the folically challenged, there is even a 'sensitive' brush with special bristles that further stimulate scalp circulation.

If cared for correctly, a Mason Pearson brush should last a lifetime. If you have spent hundreds on a haircut and highlights, it has got to be worth it!

KENT NSO1
Where? www.kentbrushes.com • All good pharmacies
How much? £8/$12/€9
The Kent NS01 nylon and pure bristle brush with wooden handle is a classic. Kent has been making brushes since 1777 and now makes over 250 models – one of which takes over 540 hours to make, a process that includes drying and hand-finishing the satinwood handle. The Kent dressing table comb also comes highly recommended.

FRÉDÉRIC FEKKAI MINI HAIRBRUSH
Where? www.fekkai.com • www.spacenk.co.uk • www.saksfifthavenue.com • www.sephora.com
How much? Approx £38/$57/€43
This Hollywood superstar hairdresser's brush is nothing short of perfection: handcrafted in France, made from natural boar bristles and tiny enough, not to say chic enough with its tortoiseshell handle, to carry around in your handbag. Perfect for one-upmanship moments in front of a communal bathroom mirror.

Lip balm

Crème de la Mer

Where?
www.cremedelamer.com • Selected department stores worldwide

How much?
Approx £35/$45/€32

Crème de la Mer

The most versatile of all beauty products, lip balm eclipses mascara in terms of its desert island must-have appeal. It is usually the first introduction to make-up a girl has, long before the joys of lipstick and eye shadow are ever allowed, and is adored by make-up artists for its ability to add lustre to cheekbones, eyelids and collarbones. A good lip balm can also smooth scaly elbows, knuckles and knees. But which is the best? Crème de la Mer may be known for producing the most expensive face cream in the world, but it is the lip balm that really shines. The pale-green balm has a lovely sludgy texture, slight minty smell and toffee-tinged taste, but it's the instantly soothing effect on chapped lips that makes it the nicest around. Not so much an everyday lip balm – but then not many of us really need lip balm every day – instead use it to indulge when your lips need some intense moisturising and tender loving care.

SISLEY NUTRITIVE LIP BALM

Where? www.sisley-cosmetics.com • Department stores worldwide

How much? £33/$70/€44

A simple pink-and-white tub holds this rich, waxy lip balm that is great for dried out, cracked lips but also as a day-to-day option. Extremely restorative, Nutritive has been designed to take special care of lips that are chapped or dehydrated by extreme weather conditions. The cocktail of natural plant extracts, including hazelnut oil, sunflower oil, shea and kokum butter, soothe the lips perfectly.

Sisley Nutritive lip balm

KIEHL'S LIP BALM #1

Where? Kiehl's stores worldwide • www.kiehls.com
How much? £7.50/$8.50/€10.00

Kiehl's legendary Lip Balm #1, first made in the late 19th century, has been a bestseller at Barneys, Bergdorf Goodman and Fred Segal for decades. It's the quality and sheer simplicity of the product – not to mention that covetable utilitarian packing – that makes it such a hit. The ingredients are all natural – sweet almond oil, vitamin E, aloe vera, wheatgerm oil and vitamin A.

> '*Just like alcohol or cigarettes, some people seem to be more susceptible to becoming dependent.*'
>
> anonymous blogger, www.kevdo.com

Kiehl's Lip Balm #1

Cult lip balms

No other beauty product has such addictive appeal – there's even an American website (www.kevdo.com/lipbalm) to help crack the lip balm habit. **Carmex** surely wins the prize for the most addictive brand. Established in 1937, the company is still family owned. The salve contains alum and salicylic acid, which was originally used to treat cold sores, and, according to Kevdo, hits you 'with a rush that rivals crack cocaine when you first apply it'.

Gwyneth Paltrow's favourite is **Smith's Rosebud Salve** – Manhattan's stylish outlet, C.O. Bigelow Apothecaries, sells more than $11,000-worth of this brand every year in mail order alone. The original Rosebud Salve, first prepared in 1892 by a Dr G. F. Smith, boasts a whole host of other uses too – it can be applied to chapped skin, blemishes, nappy rash and detergent burns. **Perfumeria Gal Madrid** is the most decorative lip balm. With its elegant Art Nouveau style packaging, this Spanish salve comes in 10 different colours and scents and is a bestseller across Europe (www.hqhair.com).

Perfumeria Gal Madrid

Carmex Balm

Mascara

Lancôme Definicils

Where?
www.lancome.com • Department stores worldwide
How much?
£19.50/$24/€26.50

Lancôme
Definicils

We all know of at least one woman who refuses to leave the house without coating her lashes in mascara. So what's the big deal? Apparently, our obsession roots back to the most basic, primal of reasons – long lashes signify good health and alertness, still attractive attributes for encouraging the opposite sex. The trick is to find a mascara that does this naturally, without clogging, smudging, flaking or irritating the eyelids. After testing as many as we could possibly get our hands on, we've come out with a clear winner: Lancôme Definicils. It's available in black, brown and the most stylish shade of all, a chic navy that goes with everything and looks good on blondes and brunettes, against black or white skin. It lengthens lashes, doesn't smudge and glides on easily. Without doubt one of the star beauty products of our time.

Yves Saint Laurent Mascara Volume Effet Faux Cils

MISS SPORTY FABULOUS LASH MASCARA

Where? www.miss-sporty.co.uk • www.superdrug.com
How much? £2.93/$4.15/€3.15

The hunt for a good, budget mascara never ceases. From the dozens tested, Miss Sporty's Fabulous Lash Mascara won hands down in this price category. Why? Because it coated lashes evenly and lasted all day without smudging. Also available in waterproof and clear.

YVES SAINT LAURENT MASCARA VOLUME EFFET FAUX CILS

Where? www.ysl.com • Department stores worldwide
How much? £21/$28.50/€23

Since launching in 2000, YSL's most popular mascara has been a massive hit thanks to its ability to make the lashes appear instantly glamorous – as if you've just applied the most perfect set of false lashes, in fact.

Best for budget lashes

Maybelline's Great Lash mascara is one of the most overrated products in the world – our testers reported smudging and flaking. Instead, for the best budget options, we recommend **Max Factor's 2000 Calorie** mascara and **Rimmel's Extreme Definition Ultimate Lash Separating mascara**, which features a unique metal wand that is more like a comb than the traditional brush and delivers a perfect application of mascara that lasts all day long.

Nail varnish

OPI Coney Island Cotton Candy

OPI Coney Island
Cotton Candy

Where?
www.opi.com • Selfridges, 400 Oxford Street, London, W1 •
00 44 800 123 400

How much?
£9.50/$8.50/€10

If there's one item of make-up that instantly makes the wearer appear ultra-groomed, it's nail polish. The polish you choose speaks volumes. Red can transform a look from plain to vixen, black says punk rock, while pearly pink says Barbie-doll cute. But what's the best? Perhaps a natural shade that looks good with pale skin or a tan, works with a casual day look or a high-octane evening do? OPI, the brand favoured by Cameron Diaz, Kate Hudson and Halle Berry, really is the best of the best. With a great consistency, it glides on nicely and stays on for days. There are a massive 250 colours to choose from with cheeky names like 'I'm Not Really a Waitress' (a striking red) and 'Can't a Berry Have Some Fun?' (a flirty fuchsia pink). The colours you put on are true to the colour you see in the bottle, so you know *exactly* what you're getting.

Essie

ESSIE
Where? www.essie.com • Selected salons worldwide
How much? £8.50/$9/€9
Essie Weingarten, a beauty industry icon, founded this brand in 1981. Available in a mouthwatering array of colours, Essie's nail polishes feature in the world's leading spas and salons, including Bliss and Canyon Ranch. Popular for their durability and chip resistance, the classic, pretty, neutral shades include Bashful Beige, Pachinko Pale and Ballet Slippers, all of which feature regularly at haute-couture shows. Madonna, Sharon Stone and Julia Roberts are fans.

PRITI
Where? www.glowgetter.co.uk
How much? Approx £12.50/$17/€13
For women who worry about the nasty chemicals, such as formaldehyde, present in most conventional nail polish, non-toxic Priti nail polish offers an alternative. Fast-drying and chip resistant, this more environmentally-friendly option also has an UV inhibitor to retain colour. Use it with the Priti Soy Polish Remover.

Priti

'It is better to apply more thin coats of polish than a few thick coats. The thicker the coat, the longer it takes to dry.'

Leighton Denny,
celebrity manicurist

Perfume

Guerlain Shalimar

Where?

68 Avenue des Champs Elysées, 75008, Paris, France • 00 33 45 62 52 57 • For other branches and stockists, visit www.guerlain.com

How much?

From £26/$46/€38

A good fragrance – a signature scent – is one that instantly sums up a woman's personality. The ultimate scent, therefore, must be distinctive; it must be relatively hard to get hold of (limited availability is always a pull); it must be French – a country that views perfumery as the most noble of art forms; and it must be a die-hard classic blend, none of that single-noted nonsense that has been popular for the past few years. A flamboyant history also helps. Shalimar from Guerlain, one of France's most prestigious perfume houses, has all of the above.

In the 1920s there was a saying – 'there are three things no respectable woman should do: smoke, dance the tango and wear Shalimar'. When it came out in 1925 the scent was described as 'racy', 'intoxicating' and 'impossibly bewitching'. Its inspiration? An epic love story from India. Three hundred years before, the emperor Shah Jahan built a beathtaking garden for his favourite wife, calling it Shalimar or 'the temple of love', and filled it with fountains, lakes, marble terraces, rare flowers and plants. But his wife died and Shah Jahan was left broken-hearted, going on to create the most beautiful mausoleum imaginable: the Taj Mahal.

In keeping with the scent's exotic inspiration, Guerlain concocted what is generally regarded as the world's first 'oriental' scent, a heady mix of bergamot, sandalwood, vetiver, patchouli and vanilla notes, the latter of which is said to have an aphrodisiac effect – no wonder it caused such a sexy stir when it first came out. Then there's the beautiful bottle with the midnight-blue stop, the pride of any dressing table. The design was originally conceived for the Decorative Arts exhibition in Paris, at a time when coloured glass was extremely unusual. The inspiration? Those exotic gardens again, as the shade is said to conjure up images of magical water.

Unlike many mass-market scents, Shalimar isn't sold everywhere, only at Guerlain's dedicated Parisian boutiques and selected department stores – Bergdorf Goodman in New York, for instance, where it has been a bestseller for more than two decades. At the Guerlain Institut on the Champs Elysées, Paris, Shalimar obsessives can buy supersized bottles, engraved with their own initials.

Dr Luca Turin, one of the best noses in the world, adores Shalimar. He's what he has to say …

'Shalimar shows that no marketing nonsense does as well in the long term as sheer beauty. The perfumery equivalent of the little black dress, the scent illustrates Guerlain's unique, effortless mastery of natural raw materials, producing a dark ashy incense joined by rich amber and a beautiful, bright and clear lemony base. As perfumer Ernest Beaux once said, "When I do a vanilla, I get cup cakes. When Jacques Guerlain does one, he gets Shalimar". It's a beauty and a timeless masterpiece.'

BOND NO. 9 CHINATOWN

Where? 9 Bond Street, New York, NY • 001 212 228 1732 • For other branches, see www.bondno9.com • www.harrods.com • www.harveynichols.com

How much? From £90/$150/€100

Launched six years ago, Bond No. 9 is a baby in perfume house terms. More eyebrow-raising still in the rarefied world of haute fragrance, the company is based in New

York – and uses the city and its neighbourhoods (from Central Park to Gramercy Park) as its muse. Yet its founder, Parisian Laurice Rahme, has all the right credentials. After working for Creed and Annick Goutal, Rahme branched out on her own, launching a range in star-shaped bottles (complete with a subway token motif, just to hammer home that New York point some more). As gimmicky as all this sounds, Bond No. 9 has been a hit with connoisseurs and customers alike. The range currently contains 26 scents – the newest, Bryant Park, is an homage to the area that hosts New York Fashion Week. Chinatown is one of the label's bestsellers, adored for its unique blend of peach blossom, gardenia, patchouli, tuberose and cardamon. A classic in the making.

FRÉDÉRIC MALLE

Frédéric Malle Lipstick Rose

Where? 37 Rue de Grenelle, 75007, Paris, France • 00 33 1 42 22 76 40 • Les Senteurs, 71 Elizabeth Street, London, SW1 • 00 44 207 730 2322 • www.editionsdeparfums.com
How much? From £70/$125/€90
Malle may be new on the scene but he has the right heritage – his grandfather helped develop the fragrance arm of his friend Christian Dior's business – as well as the right attitude, giving some of the world's best noses a free reign to create their own scents. The Paris boutique houses a number of isolation booths, where customers can smell scent in its purest form away from outside pollutants. Already iconic are Lipstick Rose and Cologne Bigarade; Chandler Burr, author of *The Emperor of Scent*, describes the latter as, 'the smell of a person in a summer thunderstorm. They are showered and clean, but it is hot, so we can smell their body, neck, clean armpits and the lovely complex smells of the summer clinging to the skin.' Blimey!

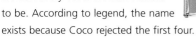

Five other cult scents

Recently there's been a revival in cult scents, the kind of fragrances that your granny used to wear and that can be instantly identified from 10 feet away. Most are cult for a reason, usually down to an interesting history and heritage. You know these will never be discontinued.

Chanel No. 5

The world's bestselling scent – there's a bottle sold every 30 seconds. It was launched in 1921 and created hysteria when it first went on sale, as it was seen as personifying Coco, the woman every other woman wanted to be. According to legend, the name exists because Coco rejected the first four.

Joy

Launched in 1927, Joy was once 'the world's most expensive perfume' (Clive Christian now claims this crown). Rather impressively, it takes over 10,000 jasmine flowers from Grasse in Provence to make a single ounce.

Rochas Femme

Made in 1944 as an exclusive scent for couturier Marcel Rochas' wife, this is a dry 'chypre' fragrance with a hint of the masculine. The bottle was inspired by the fullness of Mae West's hips.

Ormonde Jayne Frangipani Absolute

Frequently voted one of the best new scents, and made using only the finest frangipani essence – hence the purer-than-pure result. All of Ormonde Jayne's fragrances are created in-house in her London laboratory. Others include unusual ingredients like pink pepper oil and black hemlock.

Caron Tabac Blond

Along with Guerlain, Caron is another classy-yet-clever Parisian perfume house. Tabac Blond was created in 1919 and caused quite a stir thanks to its sandalwoody and somewhat masculine scent, a mix of golden tobacco, tuberose and vanilla. Utterly distinctive – a fragrance some women go batty about.

Red lipstick

Lipstick Queen Red Sinner and Saint Red

Where?

Selected department stores worldwide including Barneys New York Madison Avenue, 660 Madison Avenue, New York, NY 10021-8448 • 001 212 826 8900 • www.spacenk.co.uk • www.lipstickqueen.com

How much?

£14.68/$18/€5.79

The ancient Egyptians were the first to be seduced by the power of red lips. They used henna to paint theirs, a look that signifies strength. Red lipstick is still one of the most powerful tools in the makeup kit. Truth is, while not all reds suit everyone – and there are literally thousands of variations from flirty pink reds to siren scarlets – there are some shades – true reds, neither too blue-toned, nor yellow tinged – that suit pretty much any colouring, from pale Scandinavian complexions to olivey Mediterranean shades. Poppy King, a life-long red lipstick devotee, made it her mission to develop the ultimate red lipstick when she was just a teenager. A couple of decades on and her brand, Lipstick Queen, has a cult-following across the globe. 'I designed my Red Sinner and Saint Red to be the ultimate in true red,' explains King, who is never seen without a slick of red lipstick on her perfectly-formed pout. The best thing about this particular shade is that you can go for an intense hit by opting for Sinner, the rich opaque version, or just a hint by choosing Saint, the sheer option. Both render the wearer instantly kissable.

Lipstick Queen Red Sinner and Saint Red

'**B**eauty, to me, is about being comfortable in your own skin. That, or a kick-ass red lipstick.'

Gwyneth Paltrow, Actress

Other top reds to suit all skin shades

- **Chanel Fire #65:** A bold, true red.
- **Bésame's Red Hot Red:** A striking, bright red.
- **Guerlain's Kiss Kiss Exces de Rouge 523:** A punchy pinky red that can be worn for day or night.
- **MAC Russian Red:** A sexy, starlet red.
- **MAC Lady Danger:** An arresting, bright red.
- **Laura Mercier Seduction:** A seductive red.
- **Dior's Red Premiere 752:** A lustrous deep pinky red.

How to wear red lipstick

Poppy King, aka the Lipstick Queen, offers her expert advice:

Q: How do you know if a red suits you?
A: A red suits you if your hair, skin and eyes light up immediately. The wrong red makes you look like the sun has gone behind a cloud. The right red makes it look like the sun is shining on you.

Q: Any general tips for matching to skin and hair colour?
A: The general advice is that darker skin and hair colouring suits pinky reds and lighter skin and hair colouring suits orangey reds but I think it is about trial and error, until you hit the one that lights YOU up.

Q: How should one apply red lipstick?
A: The best way to apply red lipstick is straight from the tube, blot, allow to set and apply another coat on top. This will make it last longer.

As far as lipliner goes, only if you feel you need it, and if so then outline lips first before applying. Make sure with red lipstick that your lipliner matches the red exactly; if not then use under eye concealer around the line of the lips to stop any feathering.

Q: Who are the best red lipstick wearing icons of all time?
A: Marilyn Monroe, Ava Peron, Jerry Hall, Madonna, Chloë Sevigny.

M.A.C Ruby Woo Red

M.A.C RUBY WOO RED
Where? Department stores worldwide • www.maccosmetics.com
How much? Approx £11/$14/€12
US beauty stalwart M.A.C has built its reputation on makeup innovation – its lipsticks are among the best in terms of texture and vibrancy. No wonder this easy-to-wear bright red – leaning very slightly towards a bluish tone – is one of its best-sellers.

NARS RED LIZARD
Where? Department stores worldwide including Selfridges • www.narscosmetics.com
How much? £17/$24/€18
A modern classic, this vibrant true red delivers an instant hit of rouge. Alternatively, go for NARS popular chunky lip pencil in the same shade for a slightly more matt effect.

Nars Red Lizard

Soap

Savon de Marseille

Where?

La Compagnie de Provence, 1 Rue Caisserie, 13001, Marseille, France • 00 33 4 91 56 20 94 • www.savondemarseille.com • www.frenchsoaps.co.uk

How much?

Approx £4.50/$7/€5 per block

We're talking hand soap here, so it needs to look good on your washbasin, not as if you've been squirreling away freebies from hotels. It also needs to smell great – and work! Luckily, Savon de Marseille fits the bill on every count.

Many French women believe Savon de Marseille has magical properties, thanks to the way it is made. Indeed, Marseille has a long tradition of soap making. Its soap is made from oil, alkali from sea plants, seawater – and nothing else. No additives, no artificial colours, no animal fats, nothing. The green bars, which are scent-free, are made with olive oil, the white/beige with palm oil. Each block is stamped with the legend 'extra pur 72% d'huile garanti', a standard since 1688.

Marseille's remaining *savonneries* still use the same centuries-old method to make soap. First they brew the ingredients in cauldrons for at least ten days, rinsing repeatedly to remove any excess soda. Each block is then cut by hand – producing a satisfyingly rustic result – and left to dry naturally on racks, a process that can take months. The soap is sold by weight and each block lasts for ages. Incidentally, soap in general is currently enjoying a renaissance simply because it doesn't contain the chemicals found in some shower gels.

Savon de Marseille

AFRICAN BLACK SHEA BUTTER SOAP

Where? www.akamuti.co.uk

How much? £3.95/$6/€4.50 per bar

There are lots of shea butter imitators out there but Akamuti sells the real deal. Shea butter comes from the nuts of the karite tree, which grows wild in Africa and can't be cultivated. The production process is complicated, laborious and local; Akamuti is a Fairtrade company, so proceeds go towards helping the surrounding community. Black shea butter soap contains no preservatives or additives and aids dry skin, dermatitis and sunburn. It is also excellent for eczema – many longterm sufferers swear by it.

CLAUS PORTO SABONETE AROMATICO

Where? www.clausporto.com • www.thesoapbar.com • All good Portuguese pharmacies

How much? Approx £12/$16/€14

The Portuguese and Spanish are fanatical about soap, especially bars that come prettily wrapped and gorgeously scented. Claus Porto's creamy products, handmade in Portugal since 1887, fit the bill perfectly, and include exciting scents like Pear Sandalwood and Red Poppy. Great for gifts.

Home

'*Have nothing in your homes that you do not know to be useful or believe to be beautiful.*'

William Morris, designer, 1834—96

Alarm clock

Jacob Jensen

Where?
www.jacobjensen.com •
Various outlets including www.absolutform.co.uk

How much?
Approx £30/$45/€34

Jacob Jensen

An alarm clock is the first thing you see every morning, so it had better look good. The Danish designer, Jacob Jensen, excels in making ordinary objects – telephones and doorbells – look extraordinary. He first came to prominence as the chief designer for Bang & Olufsen, the upmarket hi-fi brand, working with them for almost 30 years, and designing more than 80 different products, before branching out on his own. Jensen is now credited with enabling us to view everyday objects with a designer's eye. It is little wonder, then, that he is represented in a number of museums around the world, among them New York's Museum of Modern Art, where he has 19 products in the Design Collection and Design Study Collection.

Jensen's alarm clock was launched in 1999. Like many of his products, the clock is characterized by its sleek lines and subdued metal colouring and has received the prestigious Red Dot award for industrial design. It looks simple, unobtrusive, and just a little bit *Star Wars*, not to say aesthetically pleasing: the LCD used to display the time has been inversed to make it look more attractive – and less obtrusive for sleepy eyes. The clock is also easy to use – it has just four keys, the concept being that one key equals one function. And for the truly lazy, a similar model is radio-controlled.

Intrepid clock connoisseurs should also head to Japan, land of the all singing, all dancing, voice-responsive mini-robotic alarm clock. The Akihabara area in Tokyo heaves under the weight of the latest in wacky wake-up technology – at surprisingly reasonable prices.

NAOTO FUKASAWA 2.5R ALARM
Where? Twentytwentyone • www.twentytwentyone.com • The Design Museum • www.designmuseumshop.com
How much? Approx £38/$54/€41
Small, perfectly formed and suitably low-fi, this analogue alarm clock (for those who prefer an old-fashioned 'tick') has a bold display and coolly functional design thanks to the Japanese industrial designer's simple aesthetic. Comes in a range of colours but black is the smartest.

LUMIE BODYCLOCK
Where? www.lumie.com • Most large department stores, including www.johnlewis.com
How much? From approx £50/$76/€56
This ingenious invention regulates the user's melatonin cycle and sleeping pattern by stimulating dawn with a gradually intensifying light. Atheletes such as the Olympic rowing champion Ed Coode use this when in training – and just think how early rowers rise.

Bed

DUX 8888

Where?
www.duxbed.com
How much? From approx £2,000/$3,050/
€2,235 for a single bed

The ultimate modern-day luxury? Getting a good night's sleep, one precious commodity that nowadays money *can* actually buy – albeit at a price. Duxiana make what has to be the ultimate bed, a

DUX Bed

combination of scientifically researched and tested mattresses – including extra springs that enable the mattress to conform to the sleeper's body shape, great when two people who prefer mattresses of differing firmnesses share a bed – with traditional wooden fittings. The Swedish company, established in 1926, crafts the kind of beds that are passed down from generation to generation, such is their durability. One of the many hi-tech details is a headboard made from northern Swedish pine, where the cold winters create super-strength wood, with controls that can be adjusted to provide support when reading. Instead of a traditional mattress, the Dux 8888 has an 'adjustable lumbar support system' complete with 'personal comfort zones'. In slightly more simple terms, this means a mattress that can be adjusted – using small cranks attached to the bed's base – and configured to suit your back, shoulders, hips and legs.

What's more, according to independent research, DUX beds are the best for inducing deep sleep, the stage necessary for proper bodily recuperation. The study noted that sleepers on a DUX bed entered the deep sleep phase faster and stayed in the state longer than they did using other beds. So it would seem that to get more sleep you really must spend more cash.

SIMON HORN SOLID EUROPEAN CHERRYWOOD LIT BATEAU
Where? 555 Kings Road, London, SW6 • 00 44 207 731 1279 • www.simonhorn.com
How much? From approx £2,900/$4,420/€3,250
Also known as a 'sleigh bed', this particular style has won a stack of design awards. Simon Horn, a former City broker based in London, is widely credited with kick-starting the renaissance of the French bed. All of his models are built by hand and are said to improve with age. Such is his cachet that Angelina Jolie is said to favour Simon Horn's cherrywood crib for her babies.

VI-SPRING
Where? www.vispring.co.uk • 00 44 1752 366311 • Stockists worldwide
How much? From £1,030/$1,600/€1,150 for a double mattress
Famous for its heavenly hand-stitched pocket-sprung mattresses that contain mohair, horsehair and silk (and equally famous for being mattress supplier to the Titanic), this venerable British company also does beds. Arguably not as pretty as Duxiana's, but built to last a lifetime.

Bed linen

Pratesi

Where?
829 Madison Avenue at 69th Street,
New York, NY 10021 • 00 212 288
2315 • www.pratesi.com

How much?
A basic 480-thread-count sheet
starts at £1,116/$1,490/€1,138

Pratesi bed linen

Enveloping oneself in crisp, white bed linen is undoubtedly the nicest way to sleep. Pratesi is synonymous with expensive bedclothes, considered by many thread-count obsessives (a thread-count is the number of threads in a one-inch square of fabric, and some of Pratesi's are well over 700) as superior to the more ubiquitous Frette. Treated properly, good bed linen is an investment that will last a lifetime – and, since we spend on average a third of our lives in bed, is definitely worth paying for. Stick to plain white or white with discreet embroidery – the 'Three Lines' embroidered Pratesi range is striking yet simple and won't date.

Pratesi is an Italian family-run company that has been going for five generations and the manufacturing of each sheet adheres to strict rules. All embroidery is done by hand, for instance, and all apprentices are taught for a minimum of five years before they are allowed to start work on any linen. But it's not just the thread count that, well, counts – of equal importance is the provenance of the cotton, the best coming from Egypt where the yarn actually gets softer and smoother with time and wear. Pratesi are super-picky and use only the top 0.002 percent.

As sheet snobs will readily attest, getting obsessed with bedding is an expensive habit and, after sleeping on a high thread-count, anything else feels like sandpaper. It's little wonder, then, that according to one Pratesi representative: 'Our hardest sell is the first-time customer. Once they buy Pratesi, they're our customers forever'.

For top-notch bed linen on a budget, try M&S's Autograph's range: fantastic quality for a fraction of the big-name price. Many interior designers swear by their sheets (www.marksandspencer.com).

FRETTE COTTON-SATIN EGYPTIAN SHEETS
Where? Montenapoleone, 21 Milan, Italy • 00 39 278 39 50 • www.frette.com
How much? From approx £332/$500/€370 per sheet
The company, founded by Edmond Frette in the French city of Grenoble in 1860, soon moved over the border to Italy where it swiftly established itself as the official supplier to the Italian royal family, as well as the Vatican. Frette's collections offer sheets with interesting borders and crocheted lace insets.

D. PORTHAULT
Where? 50 Avenue Montaigne, 75008, Paris, France • 00 33 1 47 20 75 25 • www.dporthault.fr
How much? From approx £395/$600/€440 for a set
Truman Capote once said that the difference between the rich and the rest of us was super-fresh vegetables and crisp Porthault sheets. The company was founded in 1925 when Madeline Porthault decided to introduce colour and patterns to a world of linen that was previously pure white. The label was a favourite of both Jackie and JFK and the Duke and Duchess of Windsor – both couples slept on monogrammed Porthault sets.

Blanket

Vintage Welsh wool blanket

Where?
Labour and Wait, 18 Cheshire Street, London, E2
• 00 44 207 729 6253 • www.labourandwait.co.uk

How much?
Prices from approx £75/$115/€85

Welsh wool
blanket from
Labour and Wait

OK, so the absolute ultimate may be a Hermès cashmere blanket, which costs a couple of thousand pounds and is what Kate Moss, ever the style expert, has decreed her desert island essential. But that's simply not realistic. No, the best blankets actually come from Wales. These are not nearly as soft as cashmere, but what Welsh blankets lack in pleasing tactility, they more than make up for in durability. Traditional Welsh blankets are more subtle in colour than their Scottish counterparts – the vegetable dyes used produce a softer hue – but they are just as robust, and very warm. Indeed, it is said that Welsh sheep have especially rough fleeces to combat all that rain.

Wales had a thriving weaving industry until the end of the Second World War when it could no longer compete with the larger English mills. The most covetable Welsh blankets, therefore, are the pre-1940s examples. Once found in every Welsh bedroom – the best are double-weave – they are now, alas, not quite so easy to track down, as a number of collectors have got in on the act, not to say certain designers like Ralph Lauren, who has been known to buy up old blankets and draw inspiration from their colourways.

To avoid disappointment, head to Labour and Wait, a cultish London hardware store located along a tiny East End street. The shop specializes in what it describes as 'timeless, functional products', the kind of simple goods that are nowadays almost impossible to find. The couple who own the shop scour the world for the best of the best, so the vintage Welsh blankets on sale here are better than any you'd find in Wales today. Buy one, if possible, with detachable leather straps – perfect for picnics when the weather gets warmer.

*Ralph Lauren
cashmere blankets*

RALPH LAUREN CASHMERE BLANKET
Where? For branches, see www.ralphlauren.co.uk
How much? £395/£560/€426
Woven in cable-knit and surprisingly light as well as soft and warm, this cashmere blanket is expensive but, if properly cared for, will last a lifetime. As Nigella Lawson, who has two (one for her bed; one for travelling) puts it: 'It seemed an impractical luxury at first but I've never regretted buying it.'

COLOGNE & COTTON SPOTTY THROW
Where? Branches of Cologne & Cotton • www.cologneandcotton.com
How much? £69/$98/€74
Irish blankets are lighter, and softer, than Welsh ones. This, from Cologne & Cotton, the English company that excels in beautiful blankets and bed linen, is part of a range of lambswool blankets in a host of subtle colours.

Candle

Diptyque

Where?

34 Boulevard Saint Germain, 75005, Paris, France • 00 33 1 43 26 45 27 • 195 Westbourne Grove, London, W11 • 00 44 207 727 8673 • ww.diptyqueparis.com

How much?

Approx £35/$50/€40

Diptyque Baies

Once upon a time there was potpourri – and that was it. *And* it didn't smell particularly potent. In the past few years, however, selecting the aroma of one's home has become almost as important as selecting your own signature scent, thanks in part to the trend towards cocooning. Add to that the fact that smell is the most powerful of the senses and you have a mini-revolution on your hands.

Diptyque is king of the candles. Its little glass containers, with their distinctive black-and-white typography, mark out a smart home, while a whiff of their scents is instantly recognizable as, unlike many candles, Diptyque's contain a high percentage of natural oils and essences.

The brand has long been popular with the fashion crowd – Phoebe Philo likes Pomander, while Karl Lagerfeld burns Cannelle and Héliotrope together. John Galliano, another loyal customer, has even worked with the company to produce his own scent; described as a 'warm, deep and dense fragrance with no flowers at all', it is one of the strongest smelling in the range.

The Diptyque scent that smells the most heavenly is the hot topic of many a beauty chatroom. Although popularity is somewhat seasonal – shoppers prefer spicier scents, such as Pomander (cinnamon and orange) and Feu de Bois (firewood) in the run-up to Christmas – the overall bestsellers remain Figuier (fig tree), Tubereuse (tuberose) and, at the absolute top, Baies, a combination of blackcurrant and Bulgarian rose. Such is Baies' cult status that it was the only scent chosen to be converted into a limited-edition black candle to mark Diptyque's 40-year anniversary, and die-hard, won't-burn-any-other-fragrance fans include Natalie Portman, Kylie Minogue and the supermodel Natalia Vodianova.

For the ultimate Diptyque experience, visit the original wood-panelled Saint Germain store, the address of which is etched on every bottle. Here, experienced sales staff will uncover each jar and encourage you to inhale deeply. Indeed, until as recently as 1999, this is where all the big department stores had to collect their orders from – and Lauren Bacall would actually make an annual Christmas pilgrimage to Paris simply to collect her seasonal scents.

If you still hanker for pot pourri, though, the best can be bought from the Florence-based pharmacy Santa Maria Novella, at Via della Scala 16, near the church of the same name.

BURN, BABY, BURN

To ensure you get the maximum burning time, regularly trim the wick to about 5mm before lighting and initially burn the candle for at least two hours so that the entire surface has been properly melted.

VOTIVO NO. 96

Where? www.votivo.com • Department stores and boutiques around the world
How much? Approx £16.50/$25/€19

The Red Currant edition, favourite of many a fragrant shopkeeper, has a distinctive berry scent that is pleasingly potent. Treated with care, this candle will burn for 50 hours.

CIRE TRUDON

Where? 78 rue de Seine, Paris • 00 33 143 264650 • Various international stockists such as Liberty in London and Barneys in New York • www.ciretrudon.com
How much? £45/$64/€48

The Parisian company claims to be the oldest candle-maker in the world still in operation, and has a client list (past and present) that runs from Napoleon and Marie Antoinette to Hermès and Cartier. The candles are entirely natural, with no petrochemicals, and come in a chic deep green glass complete with a gold stamp. The perfumes are natural, too, and Cire Trudon's new owner has declared a dislike for scented candles that smell in any way similar to scents used on the body. Instead, he has aimed to capture the scent of the polished wooden floors of Versailles (Roi Soleil), say, or the aroma of old stone walls found in cloisters (Carmelite).

Chic Candleholder Shopping in Copenhagen

'Hygee' (hu-gah) is a cuddly concept originating from Denmark, where it is all-pervasive, especially during the country's long, cold winter nights. The word is difficult to translate but essentially points towards a feeling of well-being and conviviality, like taking pleasure from the simple things in life such as a bottle of wine with good company. Suffice to say, the Danes are masters when it comes to atmospheric lighting, and none more so than candlelight: during the winter months, homes, shops, restaurants and bars rely on candles as a way of masking the harsh outdoor weather, lighting up as early as 9am!

Accordingly, Denmark – or, more specifically, Copenhagen – is the best place in the world to find chic candleholders.

Your first port of call should be **Illums Bolighus** (Amagertorv 10; 0045 33 14 19 41; www.illumsbolighus.com). This multi-floored department store is the ultimate in 'total design', with everything from duvets to doorstops. Candlestick names to look out for include the glass company **Iittala** (www.iittala.com), which does a fine range of colourful Aalto-inspired votive holders; and **Design House Stockholm** (www.designhouse.se) for more penny candle holders as well as the striking Nordic Light. Other noteworthy models are **Morgens Lassen's Kubus** candleholder: first realized in 1960, simple, functional, and cubic in design, it stands the test of time; ditto **Peter Karpf's Gemini** curvier candlestick (designed in 1965). Both are available from the Danish design company **Architect Made** (www.architectmade.com).

Finally, those hankering for some old-school classics should head to **Bredgade**, at the heart of the antiques district. Here you'll find pieces by **Bjørn Wiinblad**, the highly collectable and much-copied ceramicist, as well as vintage silverware from **Georg Jensen**.

Design House Stockholm candle holders

Chair

Barcelona chair, No. MR90

Where?

Aram, 110 Drury Lane, London, WC2 • 00 44 207 557 7557 • www.aram.co.uk • Knoll, Inc., 76 9th Avenue, Floor 11, New York, NY 10011 • 001 212 343 4000 • www.knoll.com

How much?

From approx £3,670/$4,329/€4,100 for basic black

Because it is the most practical and used piece of furniture, designers have always viewed the chair as an object through which they can convey their design philosophy. In 1929, the German Bauhaus designer, Ludwig Mies van der Rohe, made a chair for the Spanish king, Alfonso XIII, and his queen. It was fashioned in luxurious white leather with a steel frame and looked strikingly contemporary yet thoroughly regal, too. To this day it remains one of the most desirable chairs of all time, perhaps because it has an almost throne-like quality – it is as opulent as it is modern. Originals, dating back to before the Second World War, fetch around £10,000 each – at least three times more than later versions – and can be identified by their bent, chrome top-rail and feet with a more pronounced curve. Now reissued in a slightly simpler form and structure, with its modern but deeply masculine and luxurious shape, the Barcelona chair remains one of the most desirable pieces of furniture you can buy, the perfect combination of style and function.

Barcelona chair, No. MR90

LOUNGE CHAIR, BY CHARLES & RAY EAMES, 1956

Where? Vitra Ltd., 30 Clerkenwell Road, London, EC1 • 00 44 207 608 6200 • www.vitra.com

How much? From £4,390/$6,685/€4,900 for chair and ottoman

Charles and Ray Eames fused contemporary aesthetic with ergonomic theory to create furniture that combined the utmost in comfort with high-end materials. Created in 1956, the Lounge Chair is a modern interpretation of the traditional club chair, and is now a classic in the history of modern furniture. Finished in rosewood, faced with moulded plywood and with sumptuous leather seats, it still reeks of boardroom power and style.

MARCEL BREUER WASSILY CHAIR

Where? TwentyTwentyOne, 18c River Street, London, EC1 • 00 44 207 837 1900 • www.twentytwentyone.com

How much? From approx £1,023/$1,560/€1,150

In 1925, the German architect Marcel Breuer began experimenting with tubular steel after being inspired by his trusty Adler bicycle. The outcome was the B3, which became known as the Wassily. Its cubic proportions and the contrast between the fluidity of the steel and the tautness of the canvas – Breuer was part of the Bauhaus movement – mean that more than 80 years after its invention, it remains one of the most contemporary chairs on the market.

Jacobsen's 3107 Chair

The ultimate cult chair

With its practical plywood seat, chrome legs and simple structure, Arne Jacobsen's 3107 chair couldn't be less showy. But like many design classics, that is part of the appeal. This simple, curvy stacking chair was propelled to cult status when Christine Keeler was photographed naked and straddling a replica model in 1963. You can still buy the chair at TwentyTwentyOne (see previous page) and at Skandium (www.skandium.com). From £204/$363/€300.

Breuer's Wassily Chair

Eames Lounge Chair and Ottoman

Coffee maker

Gaggia Baby Class

Where?
www.gaggia.com • Good department stores worldwide

How much?
Approx £328/$499/€370

For the true coffee connoisseur, a good-quality coffee maker is an absolute must. There are hundreds of contraptions, including percolators, vacuum pots and fully automatic machines that administer this most potent of legal stimulants, but which comes top of the list? We found many that performed well, including Swedish brand Jura and US brand Krups, but we have honed them down to the three mentioned here, which between them include the best fully automated, the most good-looking and the most iconic.

The first espresso machine was patented in 1901 by an Italian named Luigi Bezzera, but the concept of forcing hot water through a filter of ground coffee beans wasn't developed until the late 1930s. Achilles Gaggia's purpose-built espresso machine, with a piston and lever system, was introduced in 1946 and was widely seen in 1950s coffee bars throughout Europe, so it's no surprise that one of the most superior espresso machines on the market is by this experienced brand. The Baby Class has been a hit since its launch in 1977. No wonder: it combines curvy good looks with durability and, crucially, makes a cracking cup of espresso.

Gaggia Baby Class

ILLY X1 FRANCIS ESPRESSO MACHINE

Where? www.illyusa.com
How much? £590/$900/€660

A favourite with TV and film directors because of its classic good looks, this stylish creation is manufactured by Illy, the first company to create an automatic coffee machine in 1935. With its retro styling, the Illy – designed by Italian architect Luca Trazzi – includes a pump to maintain the ideal pressure for coffee extraction, strong steam pressure for frothing milk and a brewing handle for ground coffee.

Illy X1 Francis espresso machine

LA PAVONI 'PROFESSIONAL'

Where? Via Privata Gorizia 7, 20098, Milan • 00 39 02 98 21 71 • www.lapavoni.com • Department stores worldwide
How much? From approx £580/$890/€650

It's not automatic and requires a little more patience and expertise to use, but this espresso maker from La Pavoni – a company that was founded by Desiderio Pavoni in Milan in 1903 and is credited with inventing the espresso machine – is surely one of the most loveable designs that ever adorned a kitchen.

La Pavoni 'professional'

> **' I have measured out my life with coffee spoons.'**
>
> **T.S. Eliot, poet**

KNOW YOUR COFFEE

- **Americano or lungho**: Coffee made from espresso with hot water.
- **Coretto**: An espresso with alcohol in it.
- **Crema**: A velvety thick top layer of coffee.
- **Espresso**: Literally, 'of the moment', this is the base of all good coffee. The standard shot for an espresso is 7g (⅙oz) of coffee.
- **Cappucino**: Espresso with frothy milk on the top.
- **Ristretto**: A stronger, even smaller espresso.
- **Tamping**: The process of compressing the ground coffee before the water filters through it.

COFFEE CONFIDENTIAL

- Coffee was discovered in AD 850 by an Ethiopian goat herder who noticed his goats were friskier after eating the berries from coffee bushes.
- The world's first coffee house opened in Constantinople in 1475. It wasn't until 1652 that one opened in London.
- 57 countries produce coffee in more than 100 growing regions worldwide, including Brazil, Colombia and Kenya.
- 400 billion cups of coffee are consumed annually worldwide, which means it is the world's second most sought after commodity after oil.

Coffee table

Eileen Gray E1027

Where?

Aram, 110 Drury Lane, London, WC2 •
00 44 207 557 7557 • www.aram.co.uk

How much?

From approx £575/$875/€645

Eileen Gray E1027 adjustable side table

While at first glance it seems functional and ordinary, look a little closer and the subtle sophistication of this adjustable occasional table starts shining through. Check the tinted glass top and smooth curves of the frame – sterile, stark and functional. The celebrated architect and designer, Eileen Gray, developed this timeless and modern occasional table in the 1920s, naming it after her cubist flat-roofed house on the French Côte d'Azur. And while it is not the most expensive, spectacular or decadent of tables, it is in its own quiet way the ultimate design classic, which is why it can be found in the Museum of Modern Art's permanent collection. The joy of the E1027 is that it can fit into practically any context, from a modern warehouse apartment to a small Victorian living room.

'Eileen Gray's E1027 table is among the best known examples of early 20th-century furniture design and, like all great examples of design, is both elegant and practical. When she designed the table in the late 1920s, Gray was looking forward to her sister coming to visit and, knowing that she loved breakfast in bed, designed a compact circular table specifically for that purpose.'

Alice Rawsthorn, Design Commentator

NOGUCHI IN50 COFFEE TABLE

Where? www.aram.co.uk

How much? £835/$1,191/€899

Designer Isamu Noguchi rated his coffee table, now over 60 years old and manufactured by Vitra, as his best design ever. Chunky yet elegant and perfectly balanced, it is available in either black, walnut or maple with a clear glass top.

PAPILLON COFFEE TABLE

Where? www.jensen-lewis.com • www.revoluce.co.uk
• Aram, as above

How much? £1,462/$2,440/€1,630

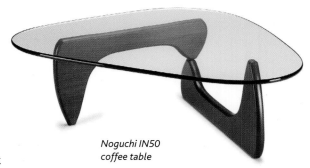

Noguchi IN50 coffee table

This sleek, double-layered, glass coffee table manufactured by Naos, which featured in the most recent *Star Wars* movie, has two adjustable surfaces, so it can work as a single unit or be flipped around to make two tables.

Cutlery and tableware

David Mellor Pride

Where?

4 Sloane Square, London, SW1 • OO 44 207 730 4259
• www.davidmellordesign.com

How much?

From approx £109/$179/€131 for a six-piece set

Utilitarian though it is, good quality cutlery, also known as flatware, enhances the look of a dining room and can impress dinner guests no end. The ultimate cutlery should be sleek, streamlined and silver. You want the fork to feel good to the touch, the knife to be a joy to cut with, and the handle of the spoon to fit snugly into the ball of your hand as you scoop up that last piece of apple pie and custard. David Mellor's award-winning 1950s-style cutlery is a fabulous investment because it has all the right credentials – elegant, sleek and smooth, and an utter pleasure to use. His sets are highly collectable, too. Sheffield-born Mellor, who passed away in May 2009, aged 78, trained as a silversmith in his teens. Drawing on the historic traditions of Sheffield cutlery, he was inspired to design the Pride range while studying at the Royal College of Art in London. It went into production in 1953, winning one of the earliest Design Centre Awards in 1957. Still manufactured in David Mellor's Derbyshire factory, and under the creative directorship of his son Corin, it has been in continuous production for over 50 years and is generally acknowledged as one of the most iconic 20th-century modernist designs. Found in stylish homes and museums across the world.

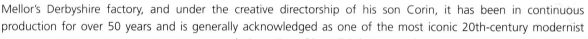

David Mellor Pride

PUIFORCAT

Where? 48 Avenue Gabriel, 75008, Paris, France • 00 33 1 45 63 10 10 • www.porcelaingalleryinc.com

How much? Five place service from approx £1,575/$2,397/€1,759

Founded by Jean Puiforcat in 1820, this elite French silversmith handcrafts cutlery to precise specifications. The silver collection spans centuries of design, from ornate and traditional French patterns to clean-lined contemporary masterpieces. The brand has recently created the elegant three-pronged fork, found in the modern Annecy range.

GIO PONTI

Where? www.etabletop.com

How much? From approx £13.34/$19/€14.42 per piece

Although he died over 30 years ago, Italian architect Gio Ponti is responsible for designing some of the most recognizable flatware around. Each piece mirrors the bold, graphics lines of his buildings.

Gio Ponti Flatware

Great for Glassware

Iittala
This Finnish company sells contemporary glassware which is functional but highly stylized.
www.iittala.com

LSA International
A 25-year-old British company specializing in contemporary, elegant glassware and particularly good for stylish giant vases. Sturdy but striking tableware and very affordable.
www.lsa-international.com

Orrefors
This highly respected Swedish glass brand made its name in the 1930s by employing artists to work on its ornamental glass production. Modern designs include the irresistably tactile 'Squeeze' collection (pictured right), designed by Lena Berström; the gorgeously chunky, space-age Marin collection by Jan Johansson; and Erika Lagerbielke's voluptuous Venus range, which is inspired by the ripples of waves. An Orrefors vase always makes a statement – even when it's free of flowers.
Skandium, 86 Marylebone High Street, London, W1, 00 44 207 935 2077, www.skandium.com

Orrefors' Squeeze vases

Pasabahçe Beykoz
Turkey's handmade glassware industry is now among the world's most innovative. Come here for Ottoman-inspired glass tableware.
Tesvikiye Caddesi, 177, Istanbul

Venini & Co
A Milanese lawyer called Pablo Venini established this glassware factory in Murano in 1921, and went on to commission high profile artists, including Salvador Dalí, to design collections in the 1930s. Venini's vintage, brightly coloured designs of the 1950s are highly desirable today, with vases fetching up to £5,050 ($10,000) at auction. The company's eternally elegant and highly collectable designs include the 707 glass vase, beautiful champagne flutes and wave-edged bowls.
San Marco, 314 Piazzetta Leoncini, Venice, Italy, 00 39 041 522 4045,www.venini.com

Classic Crockery

Thomas Goode

Dating back to 1800 and originally devised by Josiah Spode, fine bone china is a more delicate and prized alternative to porcelain. It is also the ultimate tool for keeping up with the Jones' – show it off by displaying it on dressers, in cabinets, on worktops and in kitchen cupboards for maximum effect. And if you really want to outdo the couple at number 35, start buying Thomas Goode. The British company was established in 1827 and has a history of supplying china to international royalty, including over 32 different commissions for the current British royal family alone. To this day, the small, dedicated team of craftsmen take bespoke orders and can incorporate family monograms, logos, type or even a coat of arms onto their bone china plates. Thomas Goode has also recently collaborated with Versace and Paul Smith.
www.thomasgoode.com

Thomas Goode fine bone china

Meissen of Germany became the world's first porcelain-producing factory in 1710. This porcelain can be identified by its blue sword stamp, and was sold mainly from Germany's famous china centre, Dresden, where an artistic movement encompassing art, culture, poetry, painting, philosophy – and, most importantly, china – flourished.
www.meissen.com

Spode, England's oldest pottery company was one of the first factories to use bone china. Spode is most famous for its classic 'Blue Italian' range but any of its china is highly covetable.
www.spode.co.uk

HOW TO SET A TABLE

- A table should always be laid in advance of your guests' arrival.
- You should either lay a table cloth or, if you want to show off the table, then place mats are a necessity.
- Forks should always be placed on the left of the setting with tines (prongs) facing up, while the knife (with blade facing inwards) should be placed to the right of the setting, along with any spoons that are needed.
- Spoons should only be placed above the plate when you are short on space.
- Side plates should always be placed to the left.
- Napkins should be folded simply and laid on the side plate.
- Glasses should be laid just above the knife and there should be a different wine glass for each type of wine served, plus a separate glass for water.

Desk lamp

Anglepoise

Where?
www.anglepoise.com
How much?
From approx
£128/$195/€145

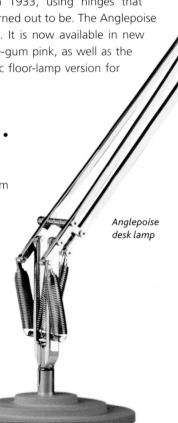

It is maybe not the most spectacular of desk lamps, but the Anglepoise is the most instantly recognizable and iconic, used by scholars, craftsmen and students the world over. Automobile engineer, George Carwardine, designed this classic in 1933, using hinges that mimicked the joint of a human arm – and what an ingenious idea it turned out to be. The Anglepoise is flexible and balanced and can be held in any position you require. It is now available in new variations including colours such as primrose yellow, aqua and bubble-gum pink, as well as the more traditional chrome, black, white or silver. There is also a gigantic floor-lamp version for those who want to play Alice in Wonderland.

TIZIO
Where? Aram, 110 Drury Lane, London, WC2 • 00 44 207 557 7557 • www.aram.co.uk
How much? £160/$245/€178
Designed in 1972, Richard Sapper's minimal, energy-efficient aluminium lamp hides the transformer in the base. This reduces voltage, which is conducted through its metal arms to power the lamp, and cleverly eliminates the need for internal wiring. With perfectly counter-balanced arms, this simple but stylish lamp is available in black, white or grey.

Anglepoise desk lamp

BLOCK LAMP
Where? Skandium, 86 Marylebone High Street, London, W1 • 00 44 207 935 2077 • www.skandium.com • www.momastore.org
How much? £153/$135/€170
Designed by Harri Koskinen for Design House Stockholm, this simple lightbulb in a block of glass has become a modern classic. A chic addition to any desk.

AND A FUN ALTERNATIVE: THE SNOOPY LAMP
Where? TwentyTwentyOne, 274 Upper Street, London, N1 • 00 44 207 288 1996 • www.twentytwentyone.com
How much? Approx £544/$828/€605
So called because it resembles a certain canine cartoon character, this lamp is bursting with personality and humour. More than simply something to illuminate the desk, the Snoopy has all the appeal of a little friend.

Fridge

FAB 28 Smeg Refrigerator

Where?
www.smeguk.com
How much?
Approximately £1,490/$2,090/€1,600

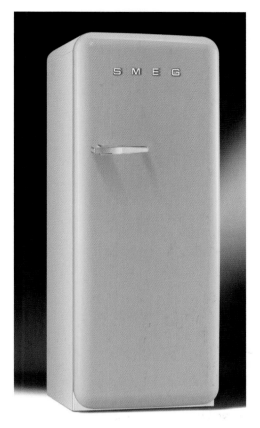

FAB 28 Smeg Refrigerator

Who would have thought that the retro-referencing Smeg fridge hasn't actually been around since the fifties, but was instead introduced to the world in 1997? It became an instant design classic, and rightly so, its bright colours and curved body making it immediately recognizable.

For domestic divas, labels in the kitchen are as important as they are for other women in the wardrobe. Smeg, therefore, is perfect: free-standing and retro, something that is very 'now' in kitchen design, and the absolute antithesis of the 1990s, when everything had to be hidden.

Smeg stands for 'Smalterie Metallurgiche Emiliane Guastalla', literally 'Metal enamelling factory based in the Reggio Emilia region of Italy', where its factories are still housed today. The company started in the late 1940s by enamelling metal products for the white goods industry. The idea for the FAB fridge came when the Smeg team noted a general yearning towards more ergonomic shapes in domestic design. They copied the distinctive rounded edges of the 1950s' American fridge, adding an enamel exterior in suitably retro shades – cream, pastel blue and pink, for instance.

The FAB is now available in 11 colours, including a Union Jack design. Something you won't want to cover with shopping lists and magnetic poetry.

SUB-ZERO
Where? www.subzero.com
How much? Prices from approx £4,800/$8,425/€7,126
Another brand that gets kitchen obsessives hot under the collar, this label is the polar opposite of Smeg: think sleek lines and a 100 percent stainless-steel body. For maximum snob appeal, choose one with a glass front, dedicated wine rack and ice-making facilities.

NORCOOL
Where? www.norcool.co.uk
How much? From approx £3,900/$5,940/€4,360
This is the closest most of us will come to an old-fashioned walk-in larder – a 'fridge pantry' with marble shelves. The Norcool has accurately, if somewhat snidely, been described as suiting the 'middle-class Volvo/Tuscany/farmers-market type who dreams of laying out his unpasteurized cheese and handmade butter on marble'.

Juicer

Champion 2000+

Where?
www.championjuicer.com • www.ukjuicers.com

How much?
Approximately £249/$245/€278

This is a juicer with a cult following thanks to its hippie roots. Champion juicers have been going since 1955, and are still made by the same family firm, based in California, a juice-friendly state if ever there was one. The 2000+ weighs a tonne, takes up too much space in the kitchen and is far from pretty, but that's not the point – it has been scientifically proven that juice from the Champion retains more nutrients from the original fruit or vegetables than any other model on the market. Which, quite frankly, is any juice-a-holic's dream. This nutrient-containing ability is due to the masticating action of the cutter – a rotating stainless-steel blade that can reach nutrients, even those locked away in the skin.

Champion 2000+ Juicer

The Champion is especially skilled with hard fruit and vegetables, is a doddle to clean, and easy to use – you simply feed through the fruit or vegetable and the pulp comes out of the other end looking rather like a 'sausage'. Despite the scores of new juicers on the market today, this is the model still cited as the best by many raw food experts.

MAGIMIX LE DUO
Where? Selected outlets including: www.amazon.co.uk
How much? From £99/$150/€110
With a centrifugal system, meaning the juicer spins the juice from the pulp, this is quiet to use – a blessing in the morning if others in the house are still asleep – looks good and comes in a range of colours. With juice bars springing up all over the shop – charging upwards of £2.50 ($4.50) a pop – the reasonably priced Le Duo makes financial sense. It even comes with a recipe book.

WARING JUICE EXTRACTOR
Where? Selected outlets including: www.everythingkitchens.com
How much? Approx £203/$310/€227
Another American brand that has been going since the 1960s, this one is easy to operate, and again, of industrial quality. It is also good with hard fruit and vegetables.

Knives

Where?

Various cookware specialists and department stores, including: www.divertimenti.co.uk

How much?

From £375/$570/€418 for a set of seven knives

Global Knives

Very sharp, very chic and very expensive, Global knives are made in Japan – a country with a history of producing sharp products; think of the samurai and their swords – and are on every kitchen snob's wish list.

The reason they're so sharp is because the blade is sharpened to a point, instead of bevelled like other knives. Another idiosyncrasy lies in the handle: received wisdom decrees that a good knife should have a 'full tang' – in other words, a blade that goes through to the handle in one piece. Global knives, however, consist of three pieces – the blade and two dimpled metal pieces that make up the handle; all welded together to create a knife that is surprisingly light. A carefully measured amount of sand inside the hollow handle provides perfect balance for the user.

Given Global's worldwide prestige, the company is relatively young, started by Komin Yamada in 1985. All knives are still made in Japan. The six-knife block is everything the amateur cook could ask for, and looks less industrial than the usual Global magnetic block.

With regular sharpening and due care – wash and dry immediately after use and never in a dishwasher – a Global knife will last a lifetime.

HENCKELS

Where? www.zwilling.com • www.divertimenti.co.uk
How much? From about £42/$64/€47 per knife
Global's closest competitors are both German companies: Wusthof-Trident and Henckels. The latter is better known and has been making knives since 1731.

LAGUIOLE

Where? www.laguiole-france.com
How much? From about £35/$54/€40 per knife
These knives, first made in 1829 in the French province of the same name, were initially used by shepherds. Today Laguiole make the best steak knives. Especially attractive is the box of six, with each handle crafted from a different type of wood, something that would make any table setting instantly eye-catching.

Light

PH Artichoke

Artichoke Light

Where?

Skandium • Ilums Bolighus in Copenhagen •

www.skandium.com•

www.illumsbolighus.com •

www.cloudberryliving.co.uk •

www.nest.co.uk • For stockists see www.louispoulen.com

How much?

Approx £4,000/$5,680/€4,305

Omnipresent in Copenhagen – and in just about any style-savvy abode – this distinctive suspension light was created in 1958 for the Danish manufacturer Louis Poulsen by Danish designer Poul Henningsen, a man obsessed with beautiful lighting.

He originally designed the Artichoke for the Copenhagen restaurant, Lagelinie Pavillionen, where it can still be found hanging today. The complex structure consists of 72 metal leaves, each one staggered over the last, which creates a filtering shield from the light source at whatever angle you stand. This staggering also reflects the light onto the underlying leaves. The end effect is a stunning piece of design that produces flattering illumination.

The Artichoke is available in white, stainless steel, and a very fetching (and surprisingly cosy) copper. Henningsen also created the iconic PH5 pendant lamp, also for Poulsen.

BAILEYS HOME & GARDEN

Where? Baileys, Whitecross Farm, Bridstow, Herefordshire • 00 44 1989 561 931 • www.baileyshomeandgarden.com

How much? From £55/$78/€59

At Baileys you are guaranteed great taste – simple, functional designs that will never date, both new and vintage. Their lights are classic and will bring a sense of texture to the room, whether it's a simple glass dome or a metal cloche.

85 BULBS CHANDELIER BY RODY GRAUMANS FOR DROOG

Where? www.droog.com

How much? £1,856/$2,633/€1,995

A bit bonkers this one, but a guaranteed talking point, 85 Bulbs is a chandelier stripped down to its bare essentials – wire, sockets and, you guessed it, 85 light bulbs. The result – from the innovative Dutch design house Droog – is masterful.

Oven

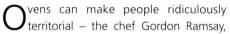

Where?
74-75 Marylebone High Street,
London, W1 • 00 44 207 258
9995 • www.aga-web.co.uk

How much?
From approx £7,000/$10,600/
€7,820

Aga Oven

Ovens can make people ridiculously territorial – the chef Gordon Ramsay, for instance, once threatened to lock his domestic model away from his wife. They can also sell houses, especially if they're an Aga, an oven that has become a byword for rural middle-class England.

Agas are special. They use radiant heat so the oven is always ready to cook; the result is that the food is moister than usual, with the flavour sealed in. An Aga's temperatures aren't readily adjustable as they are on conventional ovens; instead, cooks must rely on intuition, yet once the Aga owner understands his or her cooker's subtleties, anything is possible. Or so the theory goes. Dedicated recipe books for Aga users instruct on where certain foods can be cooked and for how long – a poppadom can be ready in seconds, for instance, by trapping it under the lid of the boiling plate.

Despite being synonymous with all things British, the Aga was actually invented in Sweden in 1922 by Dr Gustav Dalen. The aim of the Nobel Prize-winning Dr Dalen – who was blind, thus never able to see his subsequent design classic – was to create a modern cooker for his wife. Soon after his invention Agas were manufactured in Britain, a country that immediately took to the cooker's infinite possibilities, as well as its homely style.

A four-oven Aga is the most covetable – this means you can do baking and roasting separately, as well as keeping plates hot in the 'warming oven' – and is available in a range of jolly colours; Aga snobs prefer cream. Ovens come with a wire-folding toaster that can toast four slices at a time when placed on the hotplate – obsessives insist that this makes the perfect slice of toast. Agas can also be used for ironing, to open jam jars and to dry out boots … no wonder some cooks go ga-ga for Agas.

VIKING RANGE COOKER

Where? www.vikingrange.com
How much? From approx £3,282/$5,000/€3,668
The Viking doesn't have a restaurant pedigree – which is a good thing. This is a professional quality cooker designed for home cooks with the same snob-factor appeal for Americans that the Aga has for Brits. Like an Aga, a Viking range can be bought with dual ovens and comes in a range of finishes, including forest green and cobalt blue. Expect kitchen envy with one of these.

LACANCHE CLUNY STEEL RANGE

Where? Various dealers including: www.appliances.co.uk
How much? From approx £3,999/$6,090/€4,468
'The couture gown of ovens,' according to *Vogue* magazine, the Lacanche Cluny is seriously smart, with five hobs of various sizes, two ovens and storage drawers. Found in stylish urban kitchens.

Paint

Farrow & Ball New White

Farrow & Ball New White

Where?

www.farrow-ball.com

How much?

From £25/$79/€59 for 2.5 litres (0.7 gallons)

This is the new magnolia: a creamy white that is warmer than most and ideal either on its own or to complement other colours. If glossy brilliant white looks too bright, then New White is more mellow, never looking too modern nor too stark.

Part of New White's appeal is down to its pigment that includes raw umber (a natural brown clay), yellow ochre and a touch of burnt umber to give the shade warmth. The end product has a soft, almost powdery finish, something that is a trademark of posh paint-makers Farrow & Ball.

Another trademark is the company's crazy colour names: Eating Room Red (a deep, aristocratic shade), for instance, or Elephant's Breath (a soft grey). Yet it is their palette of whites for which the company is most renowned – All White, Old White, Strong White and White Tie to name but a few – and choosing exactly which one to use has driven many an amateur decorator mad. New White is the brand's bestseller, created when Off White (another popular shade and the whitest white the National Trust dared to use on the restoration of its properties), looked too grey next to regular white.

Farrow & Ball was founded in 1947, but the company really came to prominence when two old school friends, Martin Ephson and Tom Helme, bought the company in 1992. The duo revamped the brand while staying true to

Paint Tips from the Top

Kevin McCloud, the design expert and TV presenter, is also a paint obsessive. Here are his top painting tips:

- 'You can put any number of colours together, providing they are tonally similar: that is, they are equally intense or greyed, or tainted, or dirtied. What's important is that they hang out together with the same attitude.'
- 'Never underestimate the important of putting red and green together. They are complimentaries and so fire off each other, even when they are a little muted.'
- 'There is a wonderful relationship between brown and blue, better than the one between brown and green – colours that argue for the same territory on the planet. But sky and earth just seem to get on – a relationship that can be explored with many different browns and blues.'
- 'The best pinks – those that change colour under different lighting conditions – are those on the cusp of red and purple, made with red oxide pigments. The best yellows and creams – those that will withstand bluish Northern light and never look green – are those made with, or those that approximate, yellow ochre.'
- 'I'm a fan of the dado – using a band of colour on the lower part of the wall. It is a practical solution for hiding the dirt and a way of introducing strong colour to a room without overpowering it or you.'
- 'I also have to emphasize how important scatter cushions are in colour schemes. Buy them before you do anything else and then design a colour scheme around them. Paint will give you most colour choice, upholstery the least. Cushions can synthesis an entire scheme brilliantly. The same goes for rugs.'

its roots, and still manufacture all the paint they sell using traditional methods. They also use lots of pigment – up to 30 percent more than other manufacturers – resulting in a greater depth and luminance of colour.

Today Farrow & Ball is a byword for smart interior taste, the brand chosen to paint the whole of Highgrove, the Prince of Wales's estate, and mentioned in many an estate agent's details.

CRAIG & ROSE

Where? From B&Q and online and www.craigandrose.com
How much? From approx £18.58/$26/€20 for 2.5 litres (0.7 gallons)
Craig & Rose has been making paint since 1829 – and, indeed, manufactured the paint for the original Forth Bridge. As well as their traditional range, which is brimful of heritage colours, the company produces paint lines for Cath Kidston, Kelly Hoppen and Crayola. The high quality paint is water-based as opposed to solvent-based, which makes it not only better for the environment, but also easier to paint with – and clean up if mistakes are made.

THE PAINT LIBRARY

Where? www.paintlibrary.co.uk
How much? From approx £27/$41/€30 for 2.5 litres (0.7 gallons)
This excellent company will tell you which shades work best in which room, using pointers such as the amount of natural light and colour of the flooring. Tarlatan, a masculine grey shade, is one of their most popular colours.

Piano

Yamaha baby grand

Where?
www.yamaha.co.uk • www.pianoplus.co.uk
How much?
From approx £9,376/$14,280/€10,475

'No home is complete without a piano.' So said Elton John to David Beckham when giving advice on which piano he should buy as a present for his wife. Posh received a black Yamaha baby grand – Elton's favourite; he also plays on a Yamaha concert grand – with 'For My Darling Victoria' written in gold leaf under the lid.

A Yamaha baby grand is half the size of a concert grand piano. It fits into a smaller space than most baby grands as it has been designed for the modern house – only a mansion could comfortably cope with a full-sized grand piano. Yet the smaller size doesn't mean a compromise on sound. Grand pianos in general produce a better, more full-bodied sound because their strings are longer. An open lid on a grand improves the sound further letting it flood the room.

Yamaha
baby grand

Variations in sound are also linked to where the instrument was made. Yamaha pianos are said to sound fresher and crisper than the lusher, more romantic tones of those produced in Europe or the United States. Jazz musicians therefore prefer the former – both Jools Holland and the jazz legend, John Dankworth, play on Yamaha baby grands – while classical musicians plump for the latter.

YAMAHA U1
Where? www.yamaha.co.uk •
www.soundsmusical.com •
www.beethovenpianos.com
How much? From £7,074/$10,773/€7,903
If space really is an issue, then only an upright piano will do. This is regarded as one of the best – a full upright with longer strings than most, producing more of a grand-like sound.

STEINWAY MODEL B
Where? 44 Marylebone Way, London, W1 • 00 44 207 387 3199 • www.steinway.com
How much? Depending on age, material and condition, anything upwards of £20,000/$30,500/€22,350
For the snob-factor, Steinway & Sons is the ultimate brand, not to say the most expensive. Found in concert halls across the world, along with Bosendorfers and Bechsteins, Steinways are crafted using the finest materials and consist of 12,000 parts that are all made by hand – owners believe this gives each Steinway a unique soul. They are even an investment, worth more the older they become. The seven-foot Model B is most popular.

Quilt

Traditional Amish quilt

Where?
The Old Country Store, 3510 Old Philadelphia Pike,
Intercourse, PA 17534 • www.theoldcountrystore.com

How much?
Prices start at £385/$585/€430

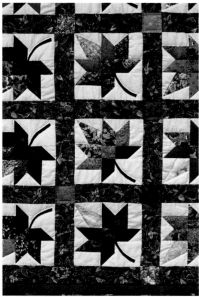

Amish quilt

The best place to find some *Little House on the Prairie*-style chic is Lancaster County in Pennsylvania, home to America's oldest Amish community and arguably the best quilters in the world.

Quilts are now the third-biggest source of income for most Amish communities, and the quilts of Lancaster County are regarded as having the finest needlework and most unusual colour combinations, often set against a darker background. Look closely, though, and you can see that the stitching isn't always super-smooth – according to lore, Amish quilt-makers deliberately mis-stitch now and then, as they believe only God can be perfect.

For the widest variety of quilts, head to The Old Country Store, housed in a Victorian-era general shop. Here you'll find hundreds of quilts, all locally made using skills that have been passed on from mother to daughter. The best quilts come from a single quilter – one pair of hands means a uniformity of stitching – and some can take up to 800 hours to make, hence the high prices. A percentage of each sale goes to the quilter.

Vintage quilts are the most covetable. In 1960s America there was a quilt revival – a natural result of the homespun hippie movement – something that has continued to this day. Nowadays, many quilts have moved from the bed to the wall, becoming bona fide museum pieces in the process, and are sometimes worth several hundred thousand dollars.

INDIAN PURE COTTON QUILTS

Where? Chunilal Mulchand, Madame Cama Road, opposite the Regal Cinema, Mumbai, India • 00 91 2202 0494
How much? From around £10/$14/€11

Since 1925, this Mumbai institution has been selling bed linen to Bombay's middle class. As well as colourful Indian quilts for a fraction of the prices found elsewhere, there are some delightful bedspreads – when we visited, we spied heavy cotton double spreads with a fan motif in retro pink, as well as elegant hand-stitched appliquéd throws from Jaipur. To complete the olde-worlde shopping experience, pay at a separate wooden booth before leaving the shop with your goods in a woven tote. A gem of a store.

ANTIQUE ENGLISH EIDERDOWN

Where? Sharland & Lewis, 52 Long Street, Tetbury, Gloucestershire, GL8 • www.sharlandandlewis.com •
The Hambledon, 10 The Square, Winchester, SO23 • www.thehambledon.com.
How much? From around £50/$76/€56

England's answer to the quilt, the eiderdown is essentially a duvet without a removable cover, so a pleasing design is a must. Antique eiderdowns are gaining cult status – and are therefore not as cheap as they once were. Find them in purveyors of shabby chic such as The Hambledon and Sharland & Lewis.

Rug

The Rug Company

Where?

124 Holland Park Avenue, London, W11 • 00 44 7229 5148 • www.therugcompany.info •
Branches worldwide

How much?

From approx £1,000/$1,523/€1,117

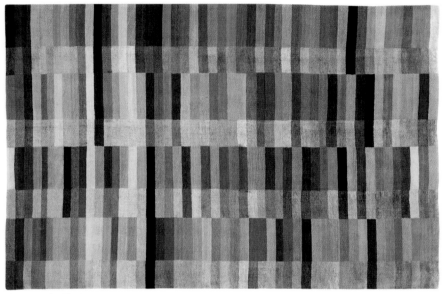

Spectrum by The Rug Company

A good rug is hard to find – something The Rug Company knows all too well. In 1997, when the business was initially launched by groovy husband-and-wife team Christopher and Suzanne Sharp, rugs were in something of a style rut: fusty, dusty, and utterly unchic. The Sharps introduced playful prints, brought big-name designers on board, and created iconic rugs in the process: Paul Smith's multi-coloured swirly number, say, Vivienne Westwood's tea-stained Union Jack, and Marni's rangy flowers. Each of the rugs is lovingly and painstakingly hand-knotted in the traditional way using hand-spun wool. The company also does limited-editions with designers such as Ron Arad, who created a memorable rug that spelt out the word 'Shag'.

The Rug Company's major role in the revival of rugs has made the Sharps design heroes: their pieces make a fantastic focal point to any room, not to say an 'investment' item. When you move home, you can roll up your Rug Company rug and take it with you. You can't do that with a fitted carpet.

KASHGAI

Where? The market in Isfahan, Iran • Liberty, Regent Street, London, W1 • 00 44 207 734 1234 • www.liberty.co.uk • Fired Earth • www.firedearth.co.uk • www.rugsuk.com

How Much? From approx £329/$500/€367 per square metre

Rugs from Persia – modern-day Iran – are still considered some of the best in the world. A dedicated rug-hunter should head to the ancient city of Isfahan, once a stop-off point for caravans travelling along the Silk Route, where thousands of rugs can still be found in piles at the market.

The best come from the Kashgai, a nomadic tribe based in southern Iran. Their rugs are hand-knotted using only the wool from the shoulders and neck of the sheep; the result is a rug that is both fine and firm. The rugs are spun by the women of the tribe and no children are involved in production, an unusual guarantee in the carpet trade. One of the reasons Iranian rugs are so good is that they are used by the same people who weave them – and they desire a quality product just as much as you do. Many sold have been used by the tribe for up to 40 years (a time-span that makes them 'antique'), but will still be in tip-top condition since they will only have been walked upon in stockinged feet. However, it is always worth checking that any wear is even and that the fringing is in a good condition.

NANI MARQUINA

Where? Stockists worldwide • www.nanimarquina.com
How Much? From £200/$291/€214
Hand-woven rugs from this Barcelona-based designer range from the classic to the super-fun. All are beautifully made and her designs are usually with a twist (excuse the pun), such as a rug made entirely from shoelaces.

Nani Marquina Victoria Rug

'**I** go to Morocco two or three times a year for inspiration. One of the best buys is rugs and carpets. I have a hoard of cream sequinned carpets – originally used as wedding blankets – that cost about £40, and I've seen them in Liberty for £250. I also invested in a proper carpet last year, a 1960s Beni Ourane. All are unique with distinctive black and white designs. In fact, World of Interiors did a piece on them recently, and although not cheap (from about £450) they're a lot less than buying them in Britain. I've seen them in London for £1,000 upwards!'

Olivia Morris, London-based shoe designer

HOW TO HAGGLE FOR A RUG

For many in Africa and Asia, bartering is a national sport. And, like any sport, there is a stringent set of rules. First, patience is crucial. The correct bartering etiquette requires time – something most merchants have in spades – as it is considered respectful to think carefully when parting with something as important as money.

Once you show even the slightest iota of interest, the game begins. Ask the price, and in a merchant's eyes you've already bought it. Sellers will start at double, triple, even ten times the amount they'd expect you to pay. Your first response should be a method-actor-worthy look of horror that is followed by a bid somewhere below half the asking price. Mentally decide on the top price you'll pay and stick with it. Once you reach it, keep repeating it over and over – the merchant will eventually get the point. And once you've both decided on a price, it is extremely rude to back out.

When dealing with antiques, ask the price first before enquiring about its provenance – that way, you'll sound like a seasoned buyer. You can also use articles you've brought from home – pens, T-shirts, etc. – as part of the deal, especially if the seller has expressed an interest.

It is also worth knowing that most merchants have their own pecking order of perceived wealth. The Japanese are charged the highest prices, then the Americans, followed by Europeans. If you are after a genuine bargain, pretend you come from some obscure country. And don't feel bad – merchants are canny and would never part with anything without turning a profit.

Sofa

Le Corbusier LC2 Sofa

Where?
www.twentytwentyone.co.uk
How much?
From
£3,184/$4,500/€3,423

Le Corbusier LC2 sofa

If a chair is the most functional piece of furniture in the house, the sofa is the most leisurely. There are thousands of styles to choose from, including grand leather Chesterfields to minimal modern varieties, but few have such style and elegance as the Le Corbusier LC2. When he wasn't revolutionizing buildings during the first half of the 20th century, the famed Swiss architect was designing radical, modern furniture to adorn those buildings. The classic, cubic two-seater, which he designed in collaboration with Charlotte Perriand in 1928, still looks as fresh and desirable as it did over 80 years ago thanks to its sleek geometric shape and chrome-plated tube cage framework featuring on the exterior. A slightly wider LC3 style is also available.

JASPER MORRISON CAPPELINI ELAN SOFA
Where? SCP Ltd • 00 44 20 7739 1869 • www.scp.co.uk
How much? From £2,706/$5,257/€7,295
Minimal and angular, the beautifully simple Elan sofa epitomizes Jasper Morrison's quiet, timeless aesthetic and would look equally chic in an English Georgian townhouse as in a modern Manhattan apartment.

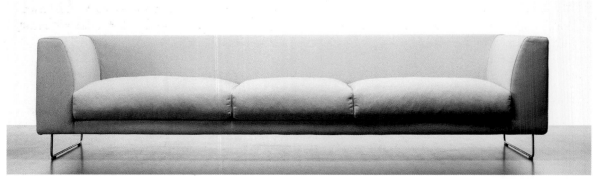

Jasper Morrison Cappelini Elan sofa

STUDIO 65, BOCCA MARILYN LIPS SOFA

Where? www.retromodern.com

How much? £2,854/$5,032/€4,184

You can't get a more inviting, provocative couch than one in the shape of a pair of juicy Marilyn Monroe lips. This 1960s Pop Art classic was a redesign of Salvador Dalí's Mae West sofa of 1936, and still looks as modern and cheeky today.

Bocca Marilyn lips sofa

Other sofa suppliers

Donghia

Angelo Donghia's furniture company displays American design at its very best. Here you'll find exuberant, impeccably made sofas that fuse classic shapes and modern styling details; for instance, the beautiful Borsalino collection, which was inspired by the Caribbean style of the 1930s and 1940s.
www.donghia.com

Mascheroni

This luxury Italian brand specializes in large, sleek leather sofas, which fuse traditional manufacturing methods with cool contemporary design. The ethos behind this brand can be summed up as passion, quality and craftsmanship.
www.mascheroni.it

Heal's

This landmark London interiors shop stocks an inspiring and affordable range of sofas, from the classic curvy Balzac range to modern modular units.
www.heals.co.uk

Three iconic sofas

Florence Knoll, Model No. 1205

This clean-lined and elegant sofa was designed in 1954 as part of Florence Knoll's quest to create the ideal 'fill-in pieces'.
www.knoll.com

George Nelson's Marshmallow sofa

Designed in 1956 with a painted tubular steel frame and vinyl-covered latex foam-filled cushions. Currently available in London at TwentyTwentyOne.
www.twentytwentyone.com

Marcel Breuer

Chromed tubular and flat steel frame with a leather upholstered seat and back cushions, this 1930s design classic has been reissued by Tecta.
www.tecta.de

Stationery

Smythson

Where?
40 New Bond Street, London, W1
and branches • 00 44 207 629
8558 • www.smythson.com

How much?
Bespoke from £187/$363/€273
for 100 cards and envelopes

*Smythson
stationery*

Stationery is having a bit of a moment. Maybe it's a reaction to the prevalence of emails, maybe a yearning back to schooldays when there was always a competition to have the best paper and pens in class. Whatever the reason, when it comes to stationery tread carefully, as the style you choose is very much a statement of how you wish the world to see you. It's all about image, about getting the right size, weight, colour and font. There are stationery snobs out there who will actually turn over letters to check the watermark. So beware.

Smythson stationery will earn you kudos. They are the Queen's favourite stationers with three royal warrants and have been used in the past by everyone from Sigmund Freud to Grace Kelly. Modern clients include Gwyneth Paltrow, who, as well as using the bespoke service, bought 20 boxes of apple-motif cards when her daughter, Apple, was born. Madonna and her daughter, Lourdes, also have their own individualized sets – the pop icon is very hot on her offspring sending 'thank you' notes, apparently.

The company was founded in 1887 when Frank Smythson started producing lightweight diaries – Princes Harry and William won't use anything else. Stationery quickly followed, as did a bespoke service, which nowadays includes hand-engraved motifs (there are over 100 to choose from, ranging from a ladybird to a black stiletto); tissue-lined envelopes in a variety of colours; hand-painted borders and different typestyles. The lettering is all hand-engraved, which means the lines are just so and the ink is of a perfect intensity. Favourite colours include Park Avenue Pink, Bond Street Blue and, of course, Nile Blue, the brand's signature shade, found on all its packaging.

BENNETON GRAVEUR

Where? 75 Boulevard Malesherbes, Paris, France • 00 33 1 43 87 57 39 • www.bennetongraveur.com
How much? From approx £35/$54/€40
Adored by Sofia Coppola, the City of Light's chicest new émigré, is smart stationer Benneton Graveur, started in 1880 by an engraver of the same name. Particularly covetable are the correspondence cards with quirky embossed motifs that include elephants, lizards and seahorses. The boutique also sells all manner of writing paraphernalia, from leather-bound notepads to signet rings.

R. NICHOLS

Where? www.r-nichols.com
How much? From approx £10/$15/€11 for a box of 8 cards
Distinctive, fashion-led designs – a typical motif is a woman rushing for a New York taxi laden down with shopping bags. R. Nichols is Manhattan based, perfect for Carrie Bradshaw acolytes everywhere.

Table linen

Busatti Melograno

Where?

14 Via Mazzini, Anghiari, Toscana, Italy, plus branches • 00 39 0575 788 013 •
www.busatti.com

How much?

Prices start at £16/$24.50/€18

Busatti Melograno

Every host or hostess needs to know how to dress a table beautifully. And, like most things, good table dressing starts with a good foundation.

Some of the most beautiful table linens can be found at Busatti. The store is an experience in itself; situated inside the pretty Tuscan walled town of Anghiari, Busatti's showrooms are housed in a vaulted 16th-century building. The family-run company was founded in 1842 and still uses the same 19th-century techniques and antique looms. All the dyes are vegetable-based and the hems are stitched by hand. The result is of a much higher quality than most of us are used to today – the fabric is soft yet washable, *very* necessary for table linen, and indeed these tablecloths are investment pieces that will last a lifetime.

Busatti's clientele include Miuccia Prada and Valentino, both fans of the company's custom-made service. Off-the-peg designs have an aristocratic feel – think plenty of jacquards in rich hues – perfect if you hanker after the stately home effect. The Melograno range (*pictured above*) feels more modern. Its fresh stripes are available in a number of colourways and the fabric is a mix of linen and cotton. Busatti also makes bed linens, which are again wonderfully soft, and upholstery materials.

BRISSI'S HEMSTITCH LINEN

Where? 22 Marylebone High Street, London, W1 • 00 44 20 7935 6733 • Brissi branches and online at
www.brissi.co.uk

How much? From £49/$69/€53 for a set of six napkins

Started by Arianna Brissi in Marlborough, England, in 2001, Brissi now has several London shops as well as an online service. The company specializes in simple hemstitch table linen made from the highest quality linen that is easy to wash, iron, and has timeless appeal.

DESIGNER'S GUILD

Where? 267 Kings Road, London, SW3 and branches • 00 44 207 351 5775 •
www.designersguild.com

How much? From £22/$33.50/24.50 for a set of four placemats

Add a splash of colour to a table of white porcelain plates with a bold print from Designer's Guild. Their signature rangy florals in citrus shades should perk up even the dullest of dinner parties.

Teapot

Mariage Frères

Where?
30 Rue du Bourg-Tibourg,
75004, Paris, France •
00 33 1 42 72 28 11 •
www.mariagefreres.com

How much?
Approx £120/$180/€135

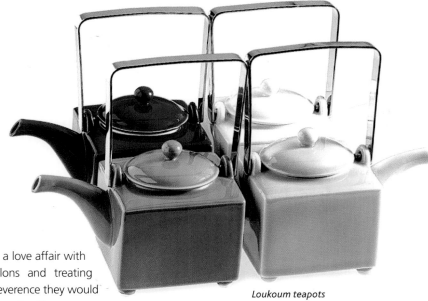
Loukoum teapots

The French are in the throws of a love affair with tea, hanging out in tea salons and treating different blends with the kind of reverence they would normally reserve for fine wine or good coffee.

So it makes sense that Paris has also become the premiere teapot-purchasing destination in the world. Mariage Frères is the city's most celebrated salon – Hugh Grant is one of many celebrity fans of this curiously olde-worlde establishment in the heart of the Marais district, and the actress Isabelle Adjani takes tea here every week.

There is a museum on the second floor, up a very creaky staircase, but the main pull is the shop itself – a veritable tea heaven, crammed with hundreds of varieties of world-class blends, including more than 50 types of Darjeeling. The teas are displayed in row upon row of canisters, ready to be dispensed into pretty little tins, the pride of any kitchen.

Also displayed in the shop's wooden cabinets are teapots, some cast iron, some porcelain, but all extremely stylish. Their Loukoum design is one of the best, a pleasing combination of Oriental wit with Western overtones in a range of striking colours: think turquoise, orange and coral. A matching Japanese-style handle-free cup is also available.

Nicolas Mariage was one of the first merchants to introduce tea to France, yet his teas have only been on sale to the general public since the 1980s; before that, only a select few, including Russia's last tsar, Nicholas II, were deemed sufficiently worthy of supping the brews. Nowadays, Mariage Frères is open to all and, since tea parties are the new cocktail parties, there's no excuse to lay a less-than-chic table.

THE BROWN BETTY
Where? From good interior shops such as Conran • online at www.edwardschina.co.uk
How much? Depending on cup-size from £8.95/$13/€10
This is a curvy classic, still made in Stoke on Trent from terracotta clay that produces a deep-brown chestnut glaze finish – and also retains the heat. Ever since the Victorian era, when tea-drinking became a popular pursuit for the masses, this has been the British pot of choice.

ARNE JACOBSEN'S CYLINDA-LINE TEAPOT
Where? Various retailers including Skandium, House of Fraser • www.scandinaviandesigncenter.com
How much? Approx £230/$326/€247
After creating the perfect chair, the Danish designer Jacobsen moved on to kitchenware and subsequently spent years creating the perfect spout for this teapot – long and dramatically upturned. As the name might suggest, all the products in his steel Cylina-Line are based on the shape of a cylinder.

Tiles

Hand-painted Portuguese azulejos

Where?
Sant'Anna Tile Factory, 96 Calcada da Boa Hora, Lisbon, Portugal •
00 351 21 363 8292 •
Sant'Anna Showroom, 95 Rua do Alecrim, Lisbon •
00 351 21 342 2537.

How much?
From approx £6.50/$9.50/€7 for a tile

Portuguese tiles

Whiz around the streets of Lisbon and you'll quickly realize that tiles *(azulejos)* are omnipresent, decorating the exteriors of the most innocuous of buildings and the interiors of everything from barbershops to butchers.

Sant'Anna is regarded as the one of the best tile producers in Europe. The company specializes in historic reproduction tiles, but will also make bespoke pieces. This traditional producer hasn't changed much in the last 200 years and all tiles are still made by hand; the pattern stencilled onto a plain white tile before being painted and then glazed. Helpful showroom staff will make your choice less time-consuming, pulling out heavy panels of completed sets so customers can see the design in its full glory. As well as reproductions, there is a small selection of antique tiles, mostly framed for use as stand-alone decorative pieces. Sant'Anna will also ship your tiles home so there's no need to worry about them weighing down your luggage.

FIRED EARTH
Where? For stockists, see www.firedearth.co.uk
How much? From around £2.50/$3.80/€2.80 per tile
Fired Earth tiles have the wow-factor and something to suit every tiling taste: from liquid glass perfect for boudoir-style bathrooms to Provençal-designs for country kitchens. To get your tiling tip-top, the devil is in the detail, something the British company knows all too well – hence Fired Earth's range of speciality grouts in subtly different tones (limestone is especially recommended) that will beautifully complement its tiles.

TALAVERA SANTA CATARINA
Where? Santa Catarina Workshop, Cholula, Puebla, 77820, Mexico • 00 52 222 247 6614
How much? From around £6.50/$10/€7.30 for a mural tile
Like Lisbon, Puebla in Mexico is a city covered in tiles. Tin-glazed 'Poblano Talavera' tiles are a speciality, although there are only a few authentic workshops left. Talavera Santa Catarina is one of them – here you'll find the real deal in bright cobalt blues, yellows, greens and ochre.

Toaster

Dualit

Where?
www.dualit.com • Various cookware specialists and department stores, including:
www.johnlewis.co.uk • www.amazon.com

How much
From approx £133/$202/€150 for a two-slice model

A kitchen classic that has spawned scores of imitators, and justly so, as the Dualit toaster does all the right things – it looks good *and* makes great toast.

The British company Dualit has been making toasters for more than 50 years and its models are a favourite with all the top hotels where a constant supply of hot toast is a must for the daily routine of breakfast. Instead of popping up, the Dualit is manually operated, switching itself off when the toast is ready and keeping it warm until you're set to add butter. The bread slots are wider than most, so they can accommodate waffles and teacakes; add a sandwich cage, and Dualit can also do a cracking toastie. Each toaster is assembled by hand and you can choose from two-, four- or six-slice options in a number of fashionable retro colours, including lavender, duck-egg blue and fire-engine red, as well as chrome.

Dualit

As if that wasn't enough, Dualit even has eco-awareness on its side, as the toasters' ability to do one slice of toast at a time with a single plate means no electricity is wasted.

SIEMENS PORSCHE DESIGN TOASTER
Where? www.siemens.com • www.johnlewis.com
How much? From approx £97.95/$149/€109
As the name implies, this slim brushed-steel model is designed by the car manufacturers. With an illuminated browning display – perfect for midnight snack sessions – and 11 levels of toasting, this two-slicer is the ultimate bachelor pad toaster.

KITCHENAID'S PRO LINE TWO-SLICE TOASTER
Where? www.kitchenaid.com • www.stylecookshop.co.uk • department stores
How Much? From approx £95/$150/€106
Desirability-wise, this brand is up there with the Dualit. As well as a pleasingly retro design, the Pro Line model has extra-wide and thick slots to fit the chunkiest of bagels.

Towels

Hammacher Schlemmer

Where?
147 East 57th Street, between Lexington and Third Avenues, New York, NY 10022 • 00 1 212 421 9000 • www.hammacher.com

How much?
Prices from £19/$30/€22

A selection of Turkish towels from Hammacher Schlemmer

What is it about fluffy white towels? Is it their cocooning quality? The super-luxe-factor? Or merely the fact that towels with a deep pile can dry you in next to no time at all – what bliss!

When it comes to quality control, towels are rather like sheets, rated by weight and provenance. Turkish-made are best, closely followed by Egyptian cotton. As for weight, the heavier they are, the deeper the pile, which makes them more effective as well as longer-lasting. Spend more, in other words, and your towels will be an investment in the long run.

Hammacher Schlemmer is a New York institution. Founded in 1848, the store has only ever had one mission: 'To find quality'. The result, thanks to their in-house institute, which researches and tests each of the products they sell, is the best the world has to offer. The towels sold here come from the Denizli region of Turkey, an area known for towelling of extraordinary thickness. They are 800g (28oz) in weight, the densest available, and with a 6mm (¼-inch) pile that means they're very, very soft.

The Manhattan-based designer Michael Kors swears by Hammacher's towels – and you know how fussy fashion folk are. 'I love the minute when my white towels are no longer white, as it means that I can simply replace them with new ones,' he says, and admits to buying new towels every three weeks for his Fire Island holiday home.

SCÉNES DE LIN

Where? 70 Rue de la Liberté, Marché du Guéliz, 4000, Marrakech, Morocco • 00 212 444 36108
How much? Prices from approx £8/$12/€9

This well-edited shop, the perfect escape from the heat, smell and dust of the souk, stocks everything a fabulously designed home could want, including giant hamam-style fringed towels. Hamam towels are generally rougher than most – all the better for a spot of exfoliation. Scenes de Lin's designs also look very stylish.

TERESA ALECRIM

Where? 76 Rua Nova do Almada, Lisbon, Portugal • 00 351 21 342 1831
How much? From £15/$27/€22

Portugal is a brilliant destination for bathroom gear – think fantastic-smelling soaps, cheap colognes and fabulous towels. *Vogue* recommends Teresa Alecrim, a place that has been described as 'Portugal's answer to Laura Ashley', for its embroidered monogrammed towels, a style popular in Lisbon.

Wallpaper

Florence Broadhurst

Where?
Signature Prints
www.signatureprints.com.au •
www.borderlinefabrics.com

How much?
Approx £230/$350/€256 per roll

We've voted Florence Broadhurst number one as her unique prints – bold designs that fuse metallic and tropical shades – have single-handedly spurred the current renaissance in wallpaper, convincing a younger paint-obsessed audience that it needn't be kitsch.

The Japanese Floral print, which features large flowers opened up like a fan, is regarded as her most iconic design, found in the New York branch of Soho House, for instance. It comes in a number of colourways including silver, aubergine, lemon yellow and bright orange. Everything is made to order and all Broadhurst papers are screen-printed by hand. Other classic prints include Imperial Brocade, a new take on classic flock, Tiger Stripes, Horses Stampede and Japanese Bamboo.

Originally from the Australian outback, Broadhurst spent some time living in Asia, where she founded an academy of modern arts, as well as Europe – she had a dress salon in Paris. After describing Australia as a 'desert that likes to buy beige', she established a wallpaper studio. Broadhurst's flamboyant lifestyle made her a minor celebrity, but it was her company that gave her kudos – she continued creating two new designs a week until her untimely death in 1977. 'My success is the fact that my wallpapers have now become a status symbol,' she once commented.

Florence Broadhurst's wallpapers lay forgotten until 1990, when her archive was discovered in a deserted warehouse. The couple behind the discovery started a company – Signature Prints – and began distributing the designs across the globe. Today, the Signature Prints team works non-stop to satisfy demand.

COLE & SON
Where? www.cole-and-son.com
How much? From approx £80/$121/€89 per roll
Exotic birds always make a popular print, and Hummingbirds from Cole & Son, a manufacturer with a royal warrant, manages to remain traditional, but not in the least bit boring. A classic.

OSBOURNE & LITTLE
Where? www.osbourneandlittle.com • Stockists worldwide
How much? From approx £45/$68/€50 per roll
Started in Chelsea, London, in 1968 by two brothers-in-law, this company is always ahead of the curve when it comes to predicting wall-covering trends (they reintroduced the flock well before most other names dared). From Japanese-inspired florals to Smartie-style dots, Osbourne & Little is a great way to create a statement wall.

Jewellery

'It would be very glamorous to be reincarnated as a great big ring on Liz Taylor's finger.'

Andy Warhol, artist, 1928–87

Cufflinks

Longmire Stirrup cufflinks

Where?
10 New Bond St, London, W1 • 00 44 207 930 8720 •
www.longmire.co.uk

How much?
From £2,500/$3,800/€2,780

For such a simple, practical accessory, it is still hard to find a truly stylish pair of cufflinks. The world seems full of tacky novelty varieties, which do a man's cuffs – and credibility – no good. Originating in the 19th century, cufflinks are a relatively new accessory for men and glide between the practical and decorative – they are as useful as a button, but double as a fine piece of jewellery.

So, where do you go for the best? Straight to Longmire, the independent English jeweller that has long been producing fine and unique cufflinks – and holds that all-important royal warrant. Inspired by the Art Deco designs of the 1930s, the stirrup style has cut sapphires mounted in solid 18-carat white gold and wraps around the edge of the cuff. Which is all very stylish indeed. The New Bond Street shop will also make a pair to your precise requirements.

Longmire Stirrup cufflinks

ASPREY 167 BUTTON PAVÉ

Where? 167 New Bond Street, London, W1 • 00 44 207 493 6767 •
www.asprey.com

How much? From approx £1,600/$2,420/€1,780

Asprey's 167-button pavé cufflinks are understated, elegant and have just a hint of bling, hailing from the shop that Elizabeth Taylor and Richard Burton frequented in their heyday. But if this style doesn't tickle your fancy, don't worry, as Asprey's fine fleet of silversmiths and jewellers are available to carry out custom-made commissions in workshops above the Bond Street premises.

Asprey 167 button pavé cufflinks

CARTIER

Where? 13, Rue de la Paix, Paris, 75002, France • 00 33 1 44 55 32 50 • www.cartier.com •
175-177 New Bond Street, London W1 • 00 44 203 147 4850

How much? From approx £3,275/$4,950/€3,645

The classic French jewellery brand specializes in diamonds. Its 18-carat yellow-gold cufflinks encrusted in the classic Cartier initials are utterly desirable.

Diamonds

Wint & Kidd

Where?

The Courtyard, Royal Exchange, London, EC3 •
00 44 207 929 1348 • www.wintandkidd.com

How much?

Price on application

In the 1944 Alfred Hitchcock film *Lifeboat*, the star isn't the gorgeous, pouting Tallulah Bankhead; instead it's a glittering Cartier diamond bracelet. When a Nazi captain discovers the piece – left by Tallulah after her boat is bombed – he ponders: 'They're really nothing but a few pieces of carbon'.

Wint & Kidd

Men, eh? They just don't get diamonds. They don't understand how a little sparkle is good for the soul; how a pair of diamond studs can magically brighten the complexion; how a diamond – a real one, that is, not a manmade rock – is a miracle of nature, each one utterly unique; why diamonds are old-school glamour; and why they really are a girl's best friend.

Thank goodness, then, that diamonds are no longer the preserve of heirloom-fortuitous blue bloods. A combination of clever marketing, accessibility – cheap internet websites, for example www.cooldiamonds.com – and bling hip-hop stars means that the diamond market is now worth £34 ($60) billion a year, the highest it has ever been. This increased popularity has also meant an increase in awareness of the appalling mining conditions suffered by most diamond workers, and certain brands, which shall remain nameless, are targets of placard-heavy protests, a somewhat incongruous sight on the world's glitzier shopping streets.

Wint & Kidd are diamond dealers with a difference. Not only do they possess an almost unrivalled selection of coloured diamonds – only one in 10,000 diamonds mined is coloured – but the company also puts money back into Angola, where they source their stones, to house, feed and educate street children. Wint & Kidd, in other words, is one of the few ethical faces in a trade riddled with human cruelty.

But ethics shouldn't be the only reason you choose Wint & Kidd. Their jewellery settings are discreet, making the most of the stone, something that is surprisingly rare in modern jewellery design, and they also make pieces to order. In addition, their shops, which are designed by Matthew Williamson, don't feel in the least bit mass-market, with helpful and knowledgeable staff on hand.

Their range of coloured diamonds is exquisite. Coloured diamonds are among some of the most valuable objects on Earth, their brilliant hues the result of impurities entering the stones as they form. The most rare are red, closely followed by green, purple, violet, orange, blue, pink and yellow. Wint & Kidd stocks them all – as well, of course, as the more usual white.

HARRY WINSTON

Where? www.harry-winston.com
How much? From £8,500/$12,865/€9,500
Established in 1932, the superstar jeweller is now synonymous
with the Academy Awards – many an actress believes his baubles
to be lucky charms. Perfect if you're looking for household-name
kudos combined with clever designs.

GRAFF

Where? 28 Albemarle Street, London, W1 • 00 44 207 584 8571
• East 61st Street, New York, NY • www.graffdiamonds.com
How much? Engagement rings from £10,000/$15,135/€11,125
'The most fabulous jewels in the world', claim the diamond-
specialists, a hyperbole that is, for once, not far off the mark.
More important diamonds have passed through Graff than

Harry Winston ring

perhaps any other dealer, from the Star of America to the 137-carat Paragon. Graff is involved with the diamond
at every stage, from the mining to the cutting and polishing, with workshops in the key diamond centres of
Antwerp and Johannesburg. They specialize in pricey – but ineffably special – engagement rings.

DEALING IN DIAMONDS

The secret to clever diamond shopping is to
understand the four Cs: carat, clarity, colour and cut.
Carat refers to the size of the diamond and clarity
refers to the flawless quality of the stone. As for the
cut, there are a number to choose from: pear, round,
marquise or princess, for instance; marquise and pear-
shaped diamonds are the most flattering on shorter
fingers. Uncut diamonds, which resemble pieces of
unpolished glass, are also known as 'rough diamonds',
and are gaining popularity as a novel way to wear the
stone. Really, what could be more decadent?

ROCK STARS

Two diamonds, in particular, deserve a mention:

The Cullinan

The biggest diamond ever was the Cullinan, which was
found in a South African mine in 1905 and weighed
3,106 carats (0.76kg/1.67lb) uncut. It was presented to
King Edward VII as a birthday gift, who chose the Asscher
brothers of Amsterdam as the cutters. It was a prestigious,
if somewhat daunting, honour – when the initial split was
performed, one of the brothers actually fainted from the
stress. The Cullinan ended up as 105 stones, the brothers
receiving 102 of them as payment. The two biggest, the
Great Star and Lesser Star of Africa, became part of the
British Crown Jewels. The pear-shaped 550.2-carat Great
Star is still the largest polished diamond in the world,
forming part of the Royal Sceptre.

The Koh-i-noor

The Koh-i-Noor, a duck-egg shaped diamond that forms
part of the British Crown Jewels, is the most famous of all
diamonds. It is by no means the biggest diamond in the
Tower of London; instead its fame derives from its tumultuous
history. According to legend, the 600-carat diamond was
discovered on the forehead of an abandoned child of the
Hindu sun god on the banks of the Yamuna River. The
gem passed from the Mughals to the Afghans to the Sikhs,
several of its owners dying to protect it. A 6th-century
valuation estimated that it was worth half the daily
expenditure of the whole world. Then, in 1849, the British
seized the stone and presented it to Queen Victoria. The
monarch had a passion for gems – she preferred wearing
her own to heirlooms – and ordered it to be cut and set
into one of her crowns.

Gems

Gem Palace

Where?
M.I. Road, Jaipur, 302001,
India • 00 91 141 2374 175
• www.gempalacejaipur.com

How much?
Price on application

Rajasthan is *the* place for gem shopping and Jaipur its epicentre, in particular the shops along Haldion Ka Rasta and Gopalji da Rasta, near the Hawa Mahal. Here you'll find men cutting and polishing stones in dusty workshops, mostly for a made-to-measure market. For a more ordered environment, head to the Gem Palace and gasp at the bowlfuls of loose gems – rubies, emeralds, diamonds, opals, aquamarines, amethysts, tourmalines and sapphires – displayed as casually as if they were candy.

Since 1852, the Kasliwal family has traded jewels to Indian royalty and celebrities like Mick Jagger, as well as European jewellery houses such as Bulgari and Cartier. Inside, the store is a veritable jewellery box. As well as loose stones, there are several ready-to-wear lines – the one by acclaimed Parisian jeweller Marie-Hélène de Taillac is especially recommended and targets Western tastes. But the real joy here is going bespoke. Simple custom-made designs can be completed in a couple of hours. It is the Indian custom to buy stones by weight and then have them

Gem Palace in Jaipur

strung – the more complex designs are usually worked upon by the Kasliwal brothers themselves. The Gem Palace also sells exquisite antique jewellery.

BERGANZA

Where? 88–89 Hatton Garden, London, EC1 • 00 44 7430 0393 • www.berganza.com

How much? From £500/$760/€556

The key to finding great antique jewellery, as opposed in trawling around endless fairs, is discovering a dealer with a fantastic eye. Berganza is such a shop: at the heart of London's jewellery quarter, the steady stream of ever-changing sparkling stock is delectable, with all important jewellery periods (Art Deco; Edwardian) amply covered.

FIONA KNAPP

Where? 178a Westbourne Grove, London, W11 • 00 44 207 313 5941 • www.fionaknapp.com
How much? Prices from approx £2,890/$4,375/€3,215

This New Zealand-born jeweller is relatively new on the scene, but has already made a significant impact with bold designs that make the most of brightly hued stones – think pink sapphires and cerise tourmalines. Her pieces are future classics.

Pink gold and pink sapphire Dandelion ring by Fiona Knapp

Oval mosaic aquamarine by Fiona Knapp

Men's rubellite cufflinks by Fiona Knapp

GLOBETROTTING GEM SHOPPING

Savvy shoppers buy their precious stones fresh from the mines, so knowing what comes from where is crucial.

Emeralds

Most come from South America, in particular Colombia. The best mines are in Muzo, Chivor and Cosquez and stones from these sites are a velvety, rich green. Bogota, the country's capital, is fast becoming the world's emerald marketing centre. Brazil, Zimbabwe, Madagascar and the Zambia, where the stones are an unusual bluish-green, are other rich sources.

Rubies

Rubies are the most valuable stone of all, and Mogok in Myanmar (Burma), an area that is known as the Valley of Rubies, is where you'll find the best in the world.

Gems

Museum and Gem Mark on Kaba Aye Pagoda Road, also in Myanmar, are reliable local dealers. Many of these gems end up in Thailand, an important centre for the ruby trade. The most prized shade is known as 'pigeon's blood red', a colour that is deep and rich.

Sapphires

These gems come in a variety of colours, including yellow and pink sapphires. A pink-orange colouring, which is known as a Padparadshah sapphire, is the most prized of all, closely followed by the cornflower-blue sapphires, which are found in Kashmir. Sri Lanka is the best place to go if you're looking for blue sapphires. Australia is currently the world's largest producer of sapphires, but these are not necessarily the prettiest – most are of an inky blue-black hue.

Gold

Dinh Van

Where?

15, Rue de la Paix, 75002, Paris, France • 00 33 1 42 61 74 49 • www.dinhvan.com

How much?

From approx £360/$545/€400 for a wedding band

Dinh Van gold band

Gold has been used in many different guises, from currency to crowns for teeth. It was first used by prehistoric man, and the oldest gold jewellery – discovered by archaeologists in the Sumerian Royal Tombs at Ur, now in Southern Iraq – is thought to date back to around 3000 BC. In 1352 BC, the young Egyptian King, Tutankhamen, was interred in a pyramid tomb laden with gold, his remains placed in an extravagant gold anthropoid sarcophagus. When the tomb was opened, it revealed an incredible 1,110kg- (2,448lb-) gold coffin and hundreds of gold and gold-leafed objects.

So what are the origins of the gold wedding band? Dating back to Egyptian times, and also used by the Romans, the ring is thought to simply resemble life and eternity. But it wasn't always so glamorous; wedding bands were simply iron hoops until the second century AD, when the true beauty, lustre and resistance of gold was fully realized.

Vietnamese-born, Paris-raised goldsmith, Jean Dinh Van, worked for Cartier in the 1950s and 1960s and now produces some of the most exquisite and luxurious gold designs in the world. The gold bands are gorgeous.

GARRARD

Where? 24 Albermarle St, London, W1 • 00 44 870 871 8888 • www.garrard.com

How much? From approx £1,000/$1,515/€1,112 for a gold band

Dating back to 1722, when original founder George Wickes entered Goldsmiths Hall, Garrard is most famous for making royal crowns. The luxury jeweller has seamlessly stepped into the 21st century and is without doubt one of the most glamorous places to go for a classic gold wedding band.

URTH JEWELLERY

Where? www.urthjewellery.com

How much? Gold pendants from approx £390/$575/€428

One of the new generation of ethical jewellery labels, Urth buy gold directly from miners and a portion of sales is reinvested back in their communities. High-profile designers Pippa Small and Stephen Webster have created exquisite ranges especially for the brand. We adore Small's Madagascan gold 'Peace Dove' pendants.

Gold for less

Istanbul, India and Greece are just a few of the countries where you can find beautifully designed gold on a budget. In Greece, A. Patrikiadou (A. Patrikiadou, 58 Pandrossou, Athens, Greece 00 30 210 325 0539) is notable for selling excellent Byzantine jewellery dating back as far as the 4th century BC. Istanbul is brilliant for buying intricately designed gold at very reasonable prices – it is just a matter of haggling a bit here and there – while Tribhovandas Bhimji Zaveri in Mumbai, India (Tribhovandas Bhimji Zaveri, 241-43 Zaveri Bazaar, Mumbai, India 00 91 22 2363 3060) has five floors of gold and gems to riffle through.

Pearls

Where?
www.mikimoto.com • www.mikimotoamerica.com

How much?
Single-strand pearl necklace from approx £1,410/$2,320/€1,570

Mikimoto

Pearl devotees are as classy as they come: think Coco Chanel and the long strings that decorated her black bouclé suits, Audrey Hepburn in *Breakfast at Tiffany's*, the Queen, and any number of chic A-Listers wearing the very *au courant* Lanvin pearls on grosgrain ribbon. Although organic in form, pearls are classed as a precious stone. They are an essential element to any jewellery box and a good set will make an outfit. But what makes a good set?

For a start, the pearl purchaser must know about natural versus cultured pearls. Only about 1 percent of all pearls are natural. These true pearls, a beauty born of irritation, are known as 'oriental pearls' and come from molluscs known as pearl oysters found mainly in the Persian Gulf, Red Sea and the Gulf of Manaar, between India and Sri Lanka. An irritant enters the oyster and is then surrounded with thin layers of nacre, or mother-of-pearl (a protein consisting of calcium) until a pearl has been formed; the thicker the layers of nacre, the more lustrous the pearl.

Mikimoto provides the best cultured-pearl necklaces, primarily because they leave the oysters alone in the nacre-building stage for the longest. The label has farmed Akoya pearl oysters since the early 1900s, assisting the conception, letting the oysters grow for two years, and then inserting a mother-of-pearl bead into the shell. The oyster is then left for at least another two years, during which time the nacre should have built up.

A velvety pink lustre makes a pearl highly prized. Other factors include the size – pearls are measured in grains – and shape; the perfect pearl should have a smooth, unblemished skin. A good quality-control test is to use your teeth – proper pearls should feel gritty when passed against them. A single strand is the most elegant and versatile; more strands are good for the evening. And it's true that regular wear is good for pearls, as they gain lustre from contact with the skin's oils. Mikimoto recently joined forces with the Japanese designer Yohji Yamamoto to produce a 29-piece collection, Stormy Weather, which takes pearls as far away from their prim-and-proper image as possible. 'A powerful mix of elegance and edge,' as Suzy Menkes from the International Herald Tribune puts it.

COLEMAN DOUGLAS PEARLS

Where? www.passion4pearls.com
How much? Necklaces start at around £110/$166/€122

Christianne Douglas, the designer behind Coleman Douglas Pearls, claims that wearing a pearl necklace is 'like an instant facelift'. When Douglas launched the label back in 1989, she transformed pearls from their dreary debutante image into something a fashion plate might covet with a line that ranges from single-strand seed pearl necklaces to South Sea and Tahitian pearls, at several thousand pounds a pop.

PASPALEY PEARLS

Where? Boutiques across Australia and in Dubai, Abu Dhabi and Hong Kong • www.paspaleypearls.com
How much? Prices start at £373/$530/€403

This Australian company was set up by the Paspaley family after seeing the success of brands such as Mikimoto in Japan, and believing they could bring the same technology to the South Seas. Which they have done, and with great aplomb: Paspaley's single pendant pearls and simple pearl stud earrings are particularly pretty.

Silver jewellery

Georg Jensen

Where?
15 New Bond Street, London, W1 • 00 44 207 499 6541 • www.georgjensenstore.co.uk •
685 Madison Avenue, New York, NY • 001 212 759 6457
How much?
From approx £100/$150/€111

Georg Jensen founded his silversmithy in Copenhagen in 1904 and quickly became known for his fine jewellery and cutlery. Simple, distinctive and strikingly modern, the 100-year-old Danish company is still easily one of the most collectable silver brands around – in fact, there's an entire website dedicated to Georg Jensen antiques (www.georgjensenantiques.com). Today, Jensen's 'Home' collection is as equally sought-after as his jewellery.

Georg Jensen bangle

Georg Jensen ring

Georg Jensen earrings

TIFFANY & CO

Where? www.tiffany.com
How much? From £225/$325/€250 for a sterling silver bangle
Established in New York in 1937 and famous for adorning Audrey Hepburn in *Breakfast at Tiffany's*, Tiffany & Co. remains one of the world's most in-demand silversmiths. Designers Elisa Peretti and Frank Gehry design highly-collectable ranges for the brand.

WRIGHT & TEAGUE

Where? 35 Dover Street, London, W1 • 00 44 207 629 2777 • www.wrightandteague.com
How much? Silver rings from £200/$300/€222
Gary Wright and Sheila Teague first met at Central Saint Martins College of Art and Design in London, and established their elegant but whimsical British jewellery brand in 1984. Stylish charm bracelets, pendant necklaces and rings inscribed with the brand's signature handwritten slogans like 'A Symbol of My Love' or, simply, 'Hope', is what makes this brand unique.

Simply Charming

The charm bracelet is possibly one of the most alluring and historical pieces of jewellery – cowrie-shell bracelets date back thousands of years, and were worn to promote fertility and wealth. Queen Victoria propelled the charm to fame by choosing to wear a cameo of her husband after his death. Today, the charm bracelet is most commonly designed in silver, and **Tiffany & Co's** (www.tiffany.com) heart-shaped sterling silver 'Heart Tag' has become one of the world's most iconic. **Links of London** (www.linksoflondon.com) offer infinite variations which can be customized – the Sloane Street store even has its own charm bar where you can pick and choose exactly what you want to go on it. Along with silver sculptures and desk accessories, Zimbabwean artist/sculptor **Patrick Mavros** (www.patrickmavros.com) creates the cutest charm bracelets featuring tiny silver animals, including lions and rhinos. We're totally smitten.

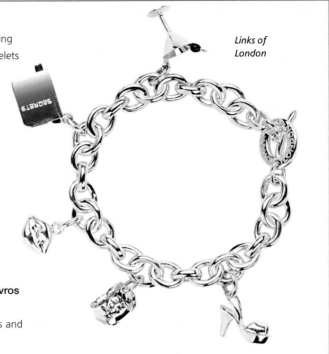

Links of London

EXPERT SILVERSMITH AND SILVER SCULPTOR, PATRICK MAVROS, GIVES THE LOW-DOWN ON SILVER SHOPPING:

How is silver different in attitude to gold?
Patrick Mavros: 'Silver is less formal, yet designed and crafted wisely it can be transformed into something more spectacular than the yellow metal. Silver is softer to look at and is often more flattering on a face or wrist than gold.'

Where does the best silver quality originate?
PM: 'Pure silver, otherwise known as fine silver, has the same quality around the world, yet the richest reefs of ore are found in the ancient mines of Central and South America.'

How is it mined?
PM: 'Either as silver-bearing ore or as a by-product of gold mining, in the same way that other metals are mined in the Earth's crust.'

Are there different grades of silver?
PM: 'Fine silver is alloyed with copper to give it strength. The end result is sterling silver. Other alloys are used depending on whether the silver will be used for enamelling or soldering.'

How can you tell if silver is of a superior quality?
PM: 'Silver must have an even, lustrous surface, with no porosity marks – these look like bubbles or stain-like blemishes. Hallmarks, the most visible sign of all, will tell you if silver is sterling or not.'

How do you clean silver?
PM: 'Most pieces of jewellery can be cleaned by rubbing them gently with a silver cleaning-cloth. These cloths are obtainable from most jewellers or stores that have silver departments. Some silver dipping solutions are also excellent cleaners. Just remember to rinse your jewellery afterwards with clean water. Silver foam can also be used.'

Watch for men

Omega Seamaster Planet Ocean Big Size

Where?
Omega stores worldwide • www.omegawatches.com

How much?
From approx £2,050/$3,100/€2,280

Selling impeccably made pocket-watches when it was established in Switzerland in 1848, Omega soon became synonymous with the most reliable watches in the early 20th century. Simple, sturdy and blessed with the ultimate seal of approval, that of Mr Bond (yes, Daniel Craig wore one in *Casino Royale*), the Omega Seamaster is a real deal man's watch. Fashioned in steel on a rubber strap, practicality is key with this design: it's water resistant to 600 metres and features a domed, scratch-resistant, sapphire crystal front.

Omega Seamaster Planet Ocean Big Size

ROLEX OYSTER

Where? Rolex stores worldwide • www.rolex.com • Watches of Switzerland, 16 New Bond Street, London, W1 • 00 44 020 7493 5916 • www.watches-of-switzerland.co.uk

How much? From approx £3,650/$5,525/€4,060

The legendary Swiss watchmaker was founded by German businessman Hans Wilsdorf in 1905. Innovations have included the self-winding watch, which was introduced in 1931 and is powered by an internal mechanism that uses the movement of the wearer's arm. All 220 of its components are assembled by hand.

BREITLING BENTLEY 6.75

Where? www.breitling.com • Watches of Switzerland (as above)
How much? Approx £5,895/$8,920/€6,560

Oozing masculinity, this chunky hunk of a watch resembles the engine of the impressive Bentley Arnage limousine that inspired its design. The Breitling was originally designed for aviation use as the extra-large face provides good visibility.

*Breitling
Bentley 6.75*

A SHORT HISTORY OF TIMEKEEPING

Early measurements of time were initially based on observations of seasonal cycles, while shorter intervals were measured by observing the shadow cast by an upright object, such as a sundial. Then came the hourglass, followed by the 'clepsydra', a water clock that measured the flow of liquid from a container. The earliest watches were ornate and date back to the 1500s, but the first mechanical, machine-made watches weren't invented until as late as the 1850s. The first modern-looking wristwatch evolved in the 1900s, although pocket watches were still popular until the Second World War when service men found smaller wristwatches more practical. Although the digital watch was invented in the 1960s, it is the classic Swiss-made dial watch that reigns as the most discerning timepiece.

Watch for women

Hermès Cape Cod

Where?

155 New Bond Street, London, W1 • 00 44 207 499 8856 • 691 Madison Avenue, New York, NY • 001 212 751 3181 • Hermès stores worldwide • www.hermes.com

How much?

From approx £1,175/$1,780/€1,305

The elegant double leather strap in classic tan or black and simple, rectangular face with a plain gold or silver frame makes this one of the most wearable and desirable watches out there. Ineffably chic.

Hermès Cape Cod

CARTIER TANKISSME

Where? 175–177 New Bond Street, London, W1 • 00 44 20 3147 4850 • www.cartier.com

How much? Approx £9,200/$13,925/€10,235

Founded in 1847 by Parisian Louis-François Cartier, the company, which is known for its diamond-studded designs, first opened a London boutique in 1902. The 18-carat-gold, diamond-set Tankissme watch (pictured on page 113) is timelessly elegant with a small square face, diamond edging and chunky white-gold silver links. Also available in a simple leather strap with a plain gold face.

EBEL BELUGA LADY

Where? www.ebel.com • Watches of Switzerland (see previous page) • Bloomingdales, 1000 Third Avenue at 59th Street, New York, NY • 001 212 705 2522

How much? Approx £3,100/$4,692/€3,450

Established in Switzerland in 1911, this luxury watch brand creates the ultimate 'jewellery' watches. The sleek and elegant 'Beluga' is set with gems – which can include diamonds, if you wish.

AND THE AWARD FOR THE MOST EXPENSIVE WATCH EVER...

Goes to Vacheron Constantin, a Swiss company founded in 1755, which became famous for its intricate skeleton-style watches in which the wearer can see all the inner workings. The Kallista watch, named after the Greek word for 'most wonderful', was made from gold ingot and set with over 130 carats of emerald-cut diamonds. It took 8,700 hours to make and sold for £4 ($6.5) million.

Shoes & accessories

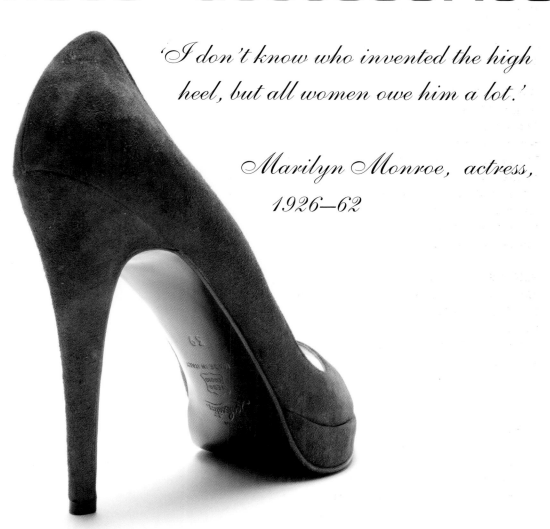

'I don't know who invented the high
heel, but all women owe him a lot.'

*Marilyn Monroe, actress,
1926–62*

Belt

Gucci GG clasp green-red-green belt

Where?
Gucci stores worldwide • www.gucci.com
How much?
£157/$295/€150

Whether it's ultra-wide, super-skinny, studded or embossed, a well-made leather belt can transform a look in one easy fastening of its clasp. And if there's one belt that transcends styles, trends and eras, it is Gucci's classic GG belt in the brand's signature green-red-green colourway. Produced by craftsmen in Tuscany, this belt was worn by supermodels and entrepreneurs in the 1980s, preppy rich American kids in the 1990s, and suave Italians since the very beginning. It epitomizes a cool, laid-back luxury. You can wear it dressed-down with jeans and a tight T-shirt, or up with a prim pencil skirt and towering heels. The message: expensive, thoroughly grown-up and properly put-together.

Gucci

HERMÈS H-CLASP BELT
Where? 175–177 New Bond Street, London, W1 •
00 44 203 147 4850 •
www.hermes.com
How much? Approx £355/$570/€410
What, exactly, is it about that sleek golden H? The classic Hermès leather belt has become a passport to instant chic. Just sling it round a pair of skinny jeans, a slim skirt or over mannish tailored trousers to add instant style and polish.

BOTTEGA VENETA LEATHER BELT
Where? Bottega Veneta stores worldwide • www.bottegaveneta.com
How much? Approx £235/$355/€260
This classic Italian brand is famed for its high-quality lattice-woven leather, producing some of the most desirable belts in the world. Each belt is hand-tooled in Italy using the softest nappa leather.

Brogues

John Lobb

Where?

9 St James's Street, London, SW1 • 00 44 207 930 3664 • www.johnlobb.com •
Also sold in over 20 countries including France, USA and Japan

How much?

Bespoke brogues from £2,000/$3,555/€2,877

No other shoe has such classic appeal as a pair of finely crafted leather brogues, and nobody does them quite like John Lobb. Established in 1866, when Lobb designed a smart pair of riding boots for the Prince of Wales and was promptly awarded a royal warrant, the brand has since become a favourite with numerous well-heeled business men and celebrities including Cecil Beaton, Somerset Maugham and, more recently, Hugh Grant and Prince Charles, all of whom appreciate the classic style and superior craftsmanship.

John Lobb

Each pair is made from the finest leather, which is cut to the anatomical dimensions of the feet, while invisible details like full-grain leather insoles, linings and stiffeners add to the comfort of the shoes. The bespoke service at the elegant, wood-panelled London store is impeccable and starts off with a measurement by a fitter, who then makes up a wooden last of the foot. A 'clicker' helps decide on the exact leather and then sends the details to the company's Northampton factory, where the shoes are hand-sewn. It is an involved process and, depending on the style of the shoes and leather required, takes varying amounts of time; one of the most unusual leathers is alligator, which can take up to four skins – and three months – to ensure consistency in the grain and texture. The most flattering brogue is Lobb's simple punched-toecap Oxford, the Philip II style. A mighty fine shoe and an investment for life, provided that you treat them with TLC.

BERLUTI

Where? 2 Rue Marbeuf, 75008, Paris, France • 00 33 1 53 93 97 97 • www.berluti.com • 43 Conduit Street, London, W1 • 00 44 207 437 1740 • Stockists worldwide
How much? From approx £2,600/$3,945/€2,900
Berluti was established by an Italian woodmaker in Paris in 1895 and make sleek, refined brogues with a distinctly Continental aesthetic.

GRENSON

Where? www.grenson.co.uk/stockists • 00 44 1933 354 300
How much? From about £110/$156/€118
Established in Northampton, the UK's shoe capital, in 1866, Grenson has long retained its reputation for providing quintessentially English brogues in the finest suedes and leathers at surprisingly affordable prices. No wonder it survived the great depression of the 1930s. Excellent value for money.

'Always use a shoehorn - it will help to keep your shoes in perfect shape. Walk your new shoes in gradually, wearing them for no more than a few hours and in dry conditions for the first few days. This allows the leather to soften and better fit your foot-shape. Rotate your pairs of shoes, so that they can dry out and breathe. If wet, leave your shoes to dry out naturally (never use an artificial heat source) on their sides so that air can circulate around both the upper and the sole. Generally, shoes will last longer if cared for properly and cleaned regularly.'

Andres Hernandez,
Production Manager at John Lobb

John Lobb

Clutch bag

Lulu Guinness fan

Where?

3 Ellis Street, London, SW1 • 00 44 207 823 4828 • www.luluguinness.com

How much?

From approx £395/$598/€440

'*Bare shoulders are a must for evening dresses and having a shoulder strap spoils the line; this is why a clutch bag is so good. As an accessories designer, I always make the bag the biggest statement of the outfit and shoes should complement but they certainly don't have to match. The worst look is when a woman wears a pale evening dress with a heavy dark quilted bag.'*

Lulu Guinness

It is neither the most fashion forward nor the most dazzling of clutch bags, but it is the most collectable, classic and utterly desirable, adored by glamazons that include Jemima Khan, Halle Berry and Sophie Dahl. Lulu Guinness' clutch fan combines humour with elegance and a dash of vintage glamour, reminiscent of old-style Hollywood. The British bag designer, who started her label in 1989 with a simple briefcase for ladies containing a bright suede lining, designed her first 'fan' bag in 1995. It subsequently sold out. Cleverly, Guinness only makes a limited number of bags, so each one becomes that much more desirable. The 'fan' is a statement in its own right – you can wear the simplest of little black dresses, yet the elegant design will add a huge helping of glamour and grace.

Lulu Guinness

JUDITH LEIBER MINAUDIERE CRYSTAL CLUTCH

Where? Department stores worldwide • 680 Madison Avenue at 61st Street, New York, NY 10065 • 00 1 212 223 2999 • www.judithleiber.com

How much? From £1,250/$1,995/€1,420

When Renée, Nicole and Scarlett are wondering which bag to take with them to their next red carpet event, there's no hesitation: a Judith Leiber minaudiere. Leiber's exquisite and expensive, gem-encrusted hard-case clutch bags spell all-out glamour.

WILBUR & GUSSIE

Where? www.wilburandgussie.com
How much? From £125/$177/€134

Launched by friends Brett Tyne and Lucy Lyons in 2005, this cute label – named after Lucy's cat Wilbur and Brett's terrier Gussie – provides humorous envelope clutches with optional wristbands and quirky clasp adornments.

Judith Leiber minaudiere crystal clutch

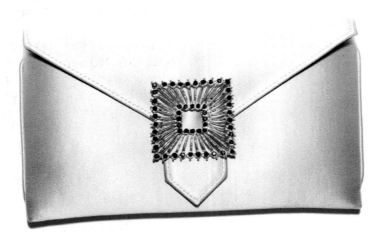

Wilbur and Gussie steel clutch

WHERE TO BAG A VINTAGE CLUTCH

Until Coco Chanel invented the handbag in 1929, the clutch ruled supreme as the elegant choice for carting your compact, lipstick and other essentials around. This means there are lots of 1920s (and earlier) clutches for vintage fiends to find – it's just a matter of knowing where to look. In London, there are some fabulous vintage bag stalls and shops full of clutches at Alfies Antique Market (www.alfiesantiques.com), Portobello Market (www.portobellomarket.org) and Islington's Camden Passage (www.camdenpassageislington.co.uk). In Paris, head to the flea market at Porte de Clingancourt (officially known as Puces de Saint-Ouen), where you'll find clutches dating back to the late 19th century. In the US, go straight to Jet Rag (825 N. La Brea Ave, Hollywood) in LA or Cherry (19 Eighth Ave) in New York's West Village for the cream of the clutch crop.

Cowboy boots

Texas Traditions

Where?

2222 College Ave, Austin, Texas, 78704 • 001 512 443
4447 • TexasTrad@aol.com

How much?

From approx £1,060/$1,600/€1,175

Texas Traditions

For the wannabe, like *Midnight Cowboy*'s Joe Buck, the allure of a finely crafted pair of cowboy boots is practically narcotic. Dating back to mid-19th century Texas, the first cowboy boots were developed with a sturdy Cuban-style heel to grip in the stirrup. It wasn't until the 1920s that cowboy boots became a fashion accessory thanks to a number of fictional cowboy characters on the radio. The increased popularity of Western movies and the men who starred in them from the 1940s onwards – particularly the likes of John Wayne – only deepened the appeal. They've been in and out of fashion ever since – worn by stars as diverse as Lenny Kravitz, John Travolta and Tom Cruise, and more recently by female fashion icons like Sienna Miller (who popularised them with her modern bohemian look), Kate Moss and Victoria Beckham.

If you are an absolute cowboy boot fiend – and, let's face it, you either love them or loathe them – where do you go for the best of the best? The answer is Texas Traditions, a company dating back over 100 years. In 1937 it famously produced the most valuable cowboy boots ever; studded with diamonds, rubies and gold, they were designed for a high-profile gambler. Now owned by Lee Miller, who took over from Charlie Dunn, Texas Traditions still makes the best quality handcrafted leather cowboy boots in the world, and has a lengthy waiting list to prove it. No wonder all the top country singers (and Sting) won't go anywhere else.

TONY LAMA

Where? www.tonylama.com • Henry Beguelin, 18 Ninth Avenue, at 13th Street, inside Hotel Gansevoort, New York, NY 10014 • 00 1 212 647 8415

How much? From approx £125/$190/€140

A hundred production stages go into making a Tony Lama boot, which is constructed to fit a wide variety of sizes in a selection of skins ranging from calf to ostrich. Each boot features a shank, a heavy gauge double-ribbed steel strip that supports the arch and is made to survive the rugged toughness of the high desert terrain around El Paso, where they are still handmade.

R SOLES

Where? 109a King's Road, London, SW3 • 00 44 207 351 5520 • www.rsoles.com

How much? From approx £225/$288/€211

Established by Douglas Berney on London's then-trendy Kings Road in 1975, R Soles quickly found a devout following of non-cowboys lusting after its fine quality cowboy boots. It remains one of the only independent shops along this famous street, offering the best cowboy boots you'll find in the UK. Designer Judy Rothchild has taken her styles to the catwalks of New York, London and Paris.

Eyeglasses

Cutler & Gross

Cutler and Gross

Where?

16 Knightsbridge Green, London, SW1
• 00 44 20 7581 2250 • Bergdorf
Goodman Men's Store, 745 Fifth
Avenue, New York • 001 800 558
1855 • selected optical stores •
www.cutlerandgross.com

How much?

From £229/$325/€246

With the advent of laser surgery and contact lenses, wearing specs has become a little like listening to vinyl or using a fountain pen: an antiquated quirk that is not entirely necessary. Still, the die-hard spec wearer knows that a great pair of glasses can be the ultimate fashion statement.

The Romans discovered magnifying glass but it wasn't until the 13th century that eyeglasses appeared in their current form, and it took a further 600 years for metal frames to emerge. Morez in the East of France became a major producer of eyeglasses and remains important with its own museum dedicated to their history. These days, spectacles are produced all over the globe and the world's most illustrious fashion brands, from Chanel to Bottega Veneta, produce their own range, but there's something more fulfilling about going to a brand that specializes purely in specs, such as Cutler & Gross. Celebrating 40 years in business in 2009, the British eyewear company has long been loved for their bold, refined frames. Current trend-setting fans include the musician Jarvis Cocker, the designer Giles Deacon and the model Kate Moss.

ALAIN MIKLI

Where? Selected optical stores worldwide • www.mikli.com
How much? From £275/$390/€295

French eyewear expert Alain Mikli has been designing cutting-edge frames for over 30 years. His handmade styles are made with cellulose acetate which contains 75 percent cotton – an ethical alternative to ivory, tortoise shell and horn. Mikli has also hooked up with designer Philip Starck to create Starck Eyes, and between them they have developed an alternative to the screw hinge: a biomechanical articulation designed like a human arm for optimum flexibility and comfort.

ANGLO AMERICAN OPTICAL

Where? www.angloamericanopticalltd.com • 00 44 20 8340 0888 • 001 800 753.9727
How much? From about £120/$170/€129

Founded in London in 1882, Anglo American Optical's distinctive frames are still handmade in the capital. With customers as diverse as Nicole Ritchie and the iconic glasses wearer Woody Allen, it is not hard to see the brand's broad appeal. The frame duplication programme means you can walk in with an old frame you want replicated.

Fountain Pen

Mont Blanc Meisterstück 149

Where?

13 Old Bond Street, London, W1 • 0044 207 629 5883 •
www.montblanc.com •

How much?

Approx £335/$505/€372

*Mont Blanc
Meisterstück 149*

The Mont Blanc Solitaire Royal pen, which is encrusted with 4,810 diamonds, is the most expensive pen ever at £70,000 ($105,000). Of course there are far cheaper alternatives – but Mont Blanc remains the brand with the most cachet.

The company was founded in Germany in 1906 and was innovative from the start, making special fountain pens with blades instead of nibs for architects and engineers during the 1920s. But its most popular style is the Meisterstück, in particular the chubby, cigar-shaped 149 model. The pen is utterly iconic and instantly recognizable – so much so that it is now on permanent display at New York's Museum of Modern Art. The Meisterstück was first introduced in 1924, and famous users include JFK and many of the recent Popes.

Made of black resin with a gold trim, the cap is topped with a signature Mont Blanc white star, a motif that represents the snow-covered summit of Mont Blanc itself. The nib is equally special, made from 18 carat gold with a platinum inlay. Each 149 passes through the hands of 120 people during its three-month production process, which includes checking the sound it makes when it hits paper and writing enough figure-of-eights to fill an A4 page. Mont Blanc has resolutely resisted the urge to use cartridges and so pens must still be filled with ink from a bottle.

The torpedo size might feel unwieldy in smaller hands; thankfully, the Meisterstück also comes in smaller sizes, all made with the same design values – the 'Classique' is a popular example. When pen shopping, you should try as many styles as possible to discover which you find most comfortable. And for the more new-school who prefer a rollerball, Acme is a fun choice. Described as the 'the Swatch of the pen business', the company has used the work of top designers past and present – Verner Panton, Frank Lloyd Wright – for its pen designs. The results are pleasingly playful. From £38.30 (www.acmestudio.com).

PARKER 51

Where? Vintage pen specialists including www.penfriend.co.uk • www.penhome.com • www.fountainpenhospital.com

How much? Depending on colourway, date, cap style and condition, from £145/$230/€164
Everyone from the composer Puccini to thousands of school children the world over has used a Parker pen. The most covetable model of this American brand is the Parker 51, introduced in 1941; like the Mont Blanc Meisterstück, it can be found in New York's Museum of Modern Art.

DUPONT ORPHEO

Where? 58 Avenue Montaigne, 75008, Paris, France • 00 33 1 53 91 30 00 • www.st-dupont.com
How much? From approx £250/$380/€280
Perhaps the most elegant range on the market, France's answer to Mont Blanc uses lush Chinese lacquers to coat their pens. Their limited editions are well worth seeking out.

> '*My two fingers on a typewriter have never connected with my brain. My hand on a pen does. A fountain pen, of course. Ballpoint pens are only good for filling out forms on a plane.*'
> Graham Greene, writer

Gloves

Sermoneta

Sermoneta

Where?
Sermoneta, 51 Burlington Arcade, London, W1 • 00 44 20 7491 9009 • 609 Madison Avenue (between 57th Street and 58th Street) New York, New York • 001 212 319 5946 • Piazza Di Spagna 61, Rome, Italy • 00 39 06 679 1960; plus other branches in Italy • www.sermonetagloves.co.uk

How much?
From £29/$41/€31

A smart pair of leather gloves is the best way to finish off a winter coat and down London's chi-chi Burlington Arcade, just off Piccadilly, you'll find the UK's first branch of Sermenta with three snug floors of hand-gear heaven: one for men's gloves, one for women's, and one for bespoke pairs. As well as London, the Italian brand, started in 1964 by husband-and-wife team Giorgio and Manuela Sermoneta, now has branches across Italy and in New York. There are literally hundreds of gloves to choose from in a rainbow of colours, scores of styles (from wrist-length to gauntlet) fashioned from leather, suede, silk and cashmere. Unlike many Italian glove-makers, Sermoneta's range often nods to seasonal trends (many we've found are stuck in a style rut, somewhere around the mid-1980s).

Rather like the fitters at Rigby & Peller – who can estimate your bra size from sight – the assistants here know your glove size at a glance. Gloves need to fit perfectly at the fingers, and new gloves should be tight-fitting as they will stretch with the shape of your hand. Prices include future repairs.

AGNELLE
Where? www.agnelle.fr
How much? From approx £90/$135/€100
This Paris-based company makes gloves for Louis Vuitton, Christian Dior, Lanvin and Celine, as well as producing its own line. Best known for stylish designs with a twist – think tassel details and bows resting on the wrist.

MADOVA
Where? Via Guicciardini, Florence, 50125, Italy • 00 39 05 52 39 65 26 • www.madova.com
How much? From approx £16/$24/€22
A family firm that was founded in Florence in 1919, Madova has gloves in every colour under the sun, at any length, both unlined and lined in wool, silk, cashmere and the warmest – albeit least animal-friendly – of all, rabbit fur. For the ultimate in glove luxury, opt for made-to-measure, which is also surprisingly affordable – around £35 ($52) for kidskin leather lined with silk.

Hosiery

Fogal

Where?

Stores and select department stores worldwide • 3A Sloane Street, London, SW1 • 00 44 7235 3115 • 515 Madison Ave on 53rd New York, NY 10022 • 001 212 355 3254 • www.fogal.com

How much?

From about £20/$29/€21.50

It was the invention of the knitting machine in 1589 that made stockings widely available. Back then, of course, they were worn by both men and women and were produced in natural fabrics only: wool, cotton and silk. Hosiery has remained a wardrobe essential ever since, holding both practical and frivolous potential. DuPont patented nylon in 1939 rendering tights/pantyhose a mass market product. One of the most desirable brands remains Fogal, a Swiss company that has been producing tights/pantyhose for more than 80 years. Selling nylons across Europe throughout the 1940s, purveying coloured opaque tights in the 1960s and now providing over 70 shades and numerous textures in its tights and stocking range, Fogal remains at the top of its game.

Fogal

WOLFORD

Where? Stores and select department stores worldwide • www.wolford.com • www.wolford-partnerboutique-w1-london.com

How much? From £11/$15.68/€11.89

This luxury Austrian company produces fine-quality legwear. With emphasis on design and innovation, top styles range from ultra-sheers to more elaborate diamond-patterned designs and intricate lacy styles in stocking, tights and legging form.

FALKE

Where? Select department stores worldwide • www.falke.com • www.figleaves.com

How much? £12/$17.12/€12.98

Established by Franz Falke in 1895, this much-loved German legwear company, originally specialized in just socks. Now the family-run business produces some of the quirkiest tights and hold-ups going, including its miraculous control top tights.

Handbag

Hermès Birkin

Where?
Hermès stores worldwide • www.hermes.com
How much?
From £3,060/$4,630/€3,405

In recent times the designer handbag has eclipsed the dress as the ultimate status symbol. And while the world's chicest women will happily shop at Zara for clothes, there is no way they will compromise when it comes to their bag – it must be as covetable and lust-worthy as can be. If there's one bag that always outshines the competition, it is the Hermès Birkin. Loved by Kate Moss, Madonna and Elle MacPherson alike, it still garners waiting lists of three months or more. The actress, Jane Birkin, inspired the creation of the first of these bags in 1984 – a supple black leather carry-all, which knocked the Kelly from the top spot due to its larger size. Now available in a variety of different

Hermès Birkin

sizes, including the popular shoulder style, which features a longer handle, the Birkin can be ordered in 8,000 different combinations of leather and fastenings. The most exclusive and expensive style ever? Perhaps the black crocodile Birkin, customized with a clasp and lock and featuring 14 carats of pavé diamonds set in white gold, which recently sold at auction in New York for a cool £35,500 ($64,800). If you want one, remortgage your house now.

Chanel 2.55

CHANEL 2.55
Where? Chanel stores worldwide • www.chanel.com
How much? From £1,200/$1,800/€1,335
It was 1929 when Coco Chanel first designed the shoulder bag; until then the clutch had ruled as the choice of elegant handbag for women, and soldiers' satchels were the only bags with straps. Chanel declared: 'I am tired of carrying my bag in my hand and losing it, so one day I added a strap and wore it as a shoulder bag.'

By 1955, she'd developed a quilted chain-strap bag, now referred to affectionately as the 'quilt and guilt', which she named the 2.55, after its birthdate – February 1955.

MULBERRY BAYSWATER

Where? Mulberry stores worldwide • www.mulberry.com
How much? £550/$650/€895

A simple, practical and quintessentially British design, this leather holdall became an instant hit when it was developed by Mulberry in 2003. The brand was established in the 1970s by Roger Saul and has become something of a cult bag label ever since. Luella Bartley hooked up with them in 2001 to create the famous Gisele bag. Thanks, in part, to the Creative Direction of Stuart Ververs, who has now left for Spanish brand Loewe, Mulberry looks set to reign as a traditional but forward-thinking British label, and its roomy Bayswater has become an all-time classic.

Mulberry Bayswater

A SHORT HISTORY OF THE 'IT' BAG

1932 Louis Vuitton Noé In signature monogram canvas, this was one of the very first cult handbags, thanks to its practical drawstring and elegant strap.

1944 LL Bean Tote Before fridges were commonly used, US brand LL Bean introduced the 'Ice Carrier' made from heavy duty canvas. It was renamed the 'Boat & Tote' in the 1960s as it became increasingly fashionable.

1958 Hermès Kelly Bag A hit when it launched in the late 1950s, this Hermès bag was renamed after Grace Kelly when she carried it around throughout her engagement to Prince Rainier. The Kelly still garners three-month long waiting lists.

1965 Gucci's 'Jackie' Shoulder Bag Simple in shape: a curved leather body with a Gucci clasp and curved shoulder strap, this bag fits snugly under the arm and became the must-have bag of the 1960s.

1996 Hervé Chapelier Travelbags These French holdalls with signature contrasting interior and exterior waterproof nylon canvas became a fashion statement during the mid to late 1990s.

1993 Kate Spade Tote The most simple of concepts: a durable, simple-shaped nylon tote that became one of the most unlikely – and best selling – accessory style hits in the US in the 1990s.

1999 Fendi Baguette A frenzy began soon after Fendi launched its now legendary baguette bag in the late 1990s. The fight was on to find new, more embellished versions, whether mirrored, sequin-scattered or appliquéd.

2002 Luella Gisele In simple tan, this satchel-inspired bag with buckles and straps became an instant best seller for Mulberry. Luella Bartley then launched new variations on the theme under her own label, Luella, in different shapes and colours, including bubble-gum pink.

2003 Balenciaga City Motocycle This neat handheld leather bag's defining feature was its wispy leather tassles. Kate Moss carried hers everywhere and her patronage helped to propel it to the height of style stardom.

2005 Chloê Paddington The slouchy leather bag with its signature weighty gold padlock shot to the top of the must-have bag super league the moment it was launched. A more compact version soon followed.

2007 Goyard Uber-ubiquitous designer bags are (for now) passé, replaced by more anonymous carry-alls by the likes of French label Goyard. So guess what's become the new must-have trophy bag? Why, Goyard's, of course, the supposedly anti-It-Bag, a point illustrated when the *New York Times'* photographer Bill Cunningham devoted an entire page to Manhattanites he'd snapped trotting out with the identikit tote. Plus ça change.

Luggage

Louis Vuitton

Where?

Louis Vuitton stores worldwide • www.vuitton.com

How much?

From £555/$960/€610 for a monogram keep-all

The two most important jobs of a suitcase? First, to hold your clothes neatly and safely, and second, to look so refined that you will have fellow travellers drooling with envy at the luggage carousel. There is no contest when choosing what will garner the biggest drools: a Louis Vuitton classic monogrammed trunk. The label, established in 1854 with the creation of its flat trunk (which remains the classiest style) has been selling its Damier canvases since 1888, and the iconic monogrammed canvas since 1896, to the super-rich from Posh and Becks to British royalty. But what, exactly, is the attraction of these cases? Perhaps the simplicity of the logo? The subdued gold-and-brown colourway? Or the chic gold clasps? It is probably a combination of all three, but there is no doubt about it: Vuitton's classic LV monogrammed canvas trunks are the most luxurious, expensive and, let's face it, ostentatious, luggage sets in the world.

Louis Vuitton trunk

GLOBE TROTTER

Where? 54–55 Burlington Arcade, London, W1 • 00 44 207 529 5950 • www.globe-trotterltd.com • For the unique bespoke cases: 00 44 207 529 5950 or email bespoke@globe-trotterltd.com

How much? From approx £195/$295/€215

Established in 1897, a Globe Trotter, with its old-fashioned charm, is the archetypal English suitcase. Their suitcases are made from Vulcan Fibre, a unique, patented material that is as light as aluminium but as hardwearing as the finest leather, and can therefore last a lifetime. Each piece is lovingly hand-crafted at the company's Hertfordshire factory by the same machines that were used in the early 1900s. Globe Trotter now offers a bespoke service that invites clients to choose from a selection of colours, exclusive Liberty-print linings, contrasting leather corners and personalized initialling.

Globe Trotter customized suitcase

Goyard Palace trunk

GOYARD'S PALACE TRUNK

Where? 233 rue St Honoré, 75001, Paris, France • 00 33 1 42 605 704 • www.goyard.fr

How much? Approx £4,560/$6,900/€5,075

Goyard was established by François Goyard in 1853, a year before Louis Vuitton, and the exquisite French company became the most sought after trunk maker in the late 19th century. François's son, Edmond, stylized the coated canvas covering with the iconic hand-painted chevron design featuring the distinctive type: Goyard Saint Honoré. Today, the original values, attention to detail and fine craftsmanship remain – each piece of luggage is still made from poplar wood, leather, fabric and beech with clasps and handles in nickel, bronze and jewels. The finishing flourish is a signature hand-painted motif that can be easily customized with the initials of those willing to pay for it. A shop has recently opened on London's Mount Street.

HOW TO PACK WITHOUT CREASING: INVALUABLE ADVICE FROM GARRY CHARNOCK, BRAND MANAGER FOR JEEVES OF BELGRAVIA, LONDON'S FINEST DRY CLEANERS

• How you fold your garments is very important. Make sure that you fold your clothes around the body pulse points – believe it or not the body heat generated around the bend of the knee, the wrists and elbows will help steam out creases when you wear them.

• Pack shoes toe to heel.

• Jersey – do not fold, just roll and then unravel for minimum creasing (this will also act as a stabilizer to fill any spaces).

• Pleated skirts and dresses – twist the pleat and pull it into a stocking to maintain the pleat.

• Double-bag all cosmetics to avoid spillage in your suitcase. Ideally, take all your cosmetics in a vanity case to protect them from damage.

• Always take laundry bags.

• Take a large canvas holdall if you intend to shop.

Pumps / Flats

Repetto

Where?
22 Rue de la Paix, Paris,
France, 75002 • 00 33 1 44
71 83 12 • www.repetto.com
How much?
From approx £150/$227/€166

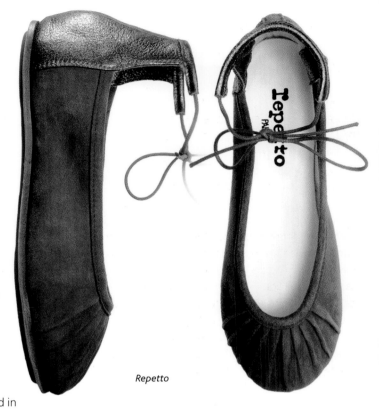

Repetto

Remember that famous image in *Working Girl* of Melanie Griffith dashing through Manhattan's financial district in an Eighties power skirt suit teamed with trainers? A couple of years ago (thanks in a giant way to Kate Moss) the ballerina pump replaced the sneaker as the comfort shoe of choice – not to say the laidback evening alternative to the stiletto. The best ballerinas are from Repetto, the original purveyors of Parisian ballerina style. Launched in 1947 by Rose Repetto – after her choreographer son urged her to start a boutique specializing in dancewear – the shoes soon picked up a devoted following from performers at Les Folies Bergère. When Brigitte Bardot wore a pair in *And God Created Woman*, Repetto pumps were transformed into a desirable fashion item. A pair of classic Repetto pumps is now a wardrobe staple, the most quintessential being the stitched-returned style, which has a leather sole sewn into the shoe inside out before being turned the right way round, ensuring the fit is super-tight (and subtly sexy). For aspiring Amélies everywhere.

FRENCH SOLE
Where? 6 Ellis Street, London, SW1 • 0044 207 730 3779 • www.frenchsole.com
How much? From approx £70/$105/€78
The 'world's largest collection' of ballet pumps – and who are we to argue? Started in 1968 in Chelsea, London, the shop experienced block-long queues when flats first came back into vogue a couple of years ago. A firm favourite with celebrities, the US First Lady Michelle Obama recently bought 10 pairs for her shoe collection.

MARC JACOBS
Where? www.marcjacobs.com
How much? From approx £83/$125/€92
Less obvious than Chanel's double-C pumps, Marc Jacobs' (or his diffusion line: Marc by Marc Jacobs) flats are great for fashion-forward wallflowers (the kind of girls Jacobs claims he prefers wearing his designs). Most styles include a small heel – more flattering than no heel at all – and that all-important toe-cleavage, while his signature 'Mouse' style has a pointed toe. Available in a fabric to suit every taste, from tweed to very-now rubber.

Sandals

K Jacques

Where?

25 Rue Allard, 83990 Saint Tropez, France • 00 33 4 94 97 41 50 • www.kjacques.fr

How much?

From approx £130/$150/€148

K Jacques

Sandals may be the simplest form of footwear, but there's a huge difference between the kind you buy for a fiver on the high street and the hand-tooled leather variety, which are properly fitted to your feet and can be found in Europe's most exclusive resorts. The ideal sandal should transport you from beach to cocktail party; it should be elegant yet practical, and show your feet off in the best possible way – complementing a tan and distracting attention from chubby chipolata toes.

The most famous sandal shop in the world, the K Jacques store in St Tropez, was established in 1933 by Monsieur and Madame Jacques Kéklikian. It was a shrewd business move: in St Tropez, sandals are as much a necessity as jeans and a white T-shirt. Their new style of made-to-measure sandals swiftly granted them a celebrity following and in the 1960s the shop shod the soles of Brigitte Bardot. Today the firm is still a family business and has three sales outlets in St Tropez, as well as a showroom that creates sandals for a wide range of the world's leading designers including Karl Lagerfeld, Missoni and Helmut Lang. With a choice of over 200 styles, you can get any shape, style or colour made up with a special bespoke service that takes just a few hours. The only additional requirement is an immaculate pedicure.

AMEDEO CANFORA 'JASMINE' JEWELLED THONG

Where? 3 Via Camerelle, near Piazzetta Quisisana, Capri, Italy • 00 39 081 837 0487 • www.canfora.com

How much? From approx £160/$245/€180

Founded by Amedo Canfora in 1946, this company is now looked after by his daughters Angela and Rita. Situated on the glitzy Italian island of Capri, this sandal shop dishes out elegant sandals to well-dressed holiday makers, from models to fashion designers, all of whom adore the handmade, jewelled, thong designs. Elegant, glamorous and distinctly Italian.

Amedeo Canfora 'Jasmine' jewelled thong

STAVROS MELISSINOS 'SOPHIA LOREN' LEATHER CORD SANDALS

Where? Melissinos Art, 2 Aghias Theklas, Athens, Greece • 00 30 210 321 9247 • www.melissinos-art.com

How much? From approx £26/$40/€29

A poet and sandal maker who has been tooling both words and leather for more than 50 years, Melissinos has made shoes for Sophia Loren and the Beatles. His 15 types of sandal can be adjusted to fit as you wait.

Scarf

Tootal

Where? From selected stockists such as www.modculture.com and www.baggamenswear.co.uk

How much?

From approx £35/$50/€38

Men's scarves have a huge and varied history: they are evident on ancient Chinese sculptures; the Romans later wore something called a sudarium, which was a linen kerchief; and in 17th-century Britain, no man would be seen dead without an elegant silk number. Widening and protecting the neck, it was considered to reinforce masculinity and was adopted by women much later on. Recently, along with bespoke suits, brogues and silk socks, the silk scarf has made something of a comeback. A scarf is gentlemanly, luxurious and a sign of refinement. Established in 1799, British brand Tootal delivers dandyish silk scarves with tassles, as favoured by Mods in the 1960s. The heritage brand's designs remain strikingly similar to the initial styles of 200 years ago – although the current range revisits old patterns in bold new colourways. Fans include Paul Weller, The Kaiser Chiefs and the Gallagher brothers.

Tootal scarves

DUCHAMP

Where? 155 Regent Street, London, W1 • 00 44 207 494 0333 • www.duchamplondon.co.uk

How much? From approx £100/$150/€110

The quirky London-based company, famous for its vibrant men's accessories, delivers a selection of ultra-dapper and brightly coloured variations on the classic silk scarf.

ETRO

Where? 14 Old Bond St, London, W1 • 00 44 207 495 5767 • www.etro.it

How much? From approx £110/$165/€122

The Italian brand famous for its sharp suits and shirts in vivid shades also designs smart silk scarves for the modern-day dandy, not to say coloured pashminas for men.

Slippers

Pia Wallén

Where?

From selected stockists such as Skandium, www.skandium.com. For more information, visit www.piawallen.com

How Much?

Approx £39/$59/€44

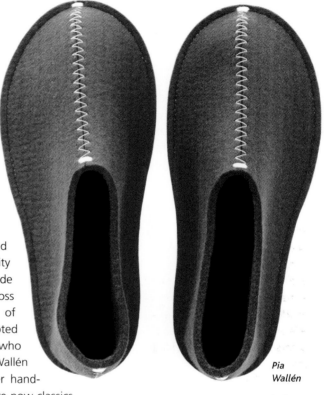

Pia Wallén

Coming from a place where it's dark most of the year, the Scandinavians know a thing or two about comfort. They also know a thing or two about style, making Pia Wallén's wool felt slippers the best when it comes to keeping your toes toasty.

Wallén is an award-winning Stockholm-based interior designer who started working in high-quality felt – and never really wavered. Her slippers are made from just that, with contrasting zig-zag stitching across the toe and rubber soles, available in a number of pleasingly bright colourways and styles. The full-footed affair, for instance, is perfect for the kind of people who don't want their slippers to look like, well, slippers. Wallén also makes a range of rugs, blankets, pillows – her hand-woven wool throws with a cross motif, 'The Crux', are now classics. And while we're on the subject of slipper shopping in chilly climes, super-warm Mongolian slip-ons made from yak leather and camel hair also come highly recommended.

BELDI BABOUCHES

Where? Beldi, 9–11 Souikat Laksour, Medina, Marrakech, Morocco • 00 212 44 441 076

How much? From approx £40/$60/€45

Moroccan babouches are *the* smart slipper choice. The pointy-toed version was invented in the Moroccan city of Fez, where distinctive yellow and white slippers are still made today for the royal household. Those with a rounder toe – less severe and more aesthetically pleasing – are from Marrakech, the smartest from Beldi, a boutique that flawlessly blends oriental craftsmanship with occidental taste. Beldi's babouches are more expensive than most but worth it since they're hand-sewn in the finest leather. Jean Paul Gaultier is a fan – he has a riad in the medina – as are many of his fellow fashion jetsetters. Le Souk des Babouches is dedicated to slippers but watch out for quality – the soles should be stitched, not glued.

SHEEPSKIN SCUFFS

Where? www.sheepskinscuffs.com • www.hush-uk.com

How much? From approx £45/$68/€50

From the same brain that brought you the Ugg boot, Scuffs are crafted from soft suede with a toe-pleasing sheepskin lining. Perfect for chilly winter's nights when only sheepskin will do.

Socks

Pantherella

Where?
www.pantherella.co.uk
How much?
From approx £9.50/$14/€10.50 per pair

For many men, socks are something of a trademark. Think about it: suited and booted, how else are they going to stand out from the corporate crowd? Pantherella, a company based in Leicester, has been going for over 65 years and is generally considered the best sock-maker in the world – if you are buying your suit from Savile Row, Pantherella is where you'll purchase your socks.

Pantherella

The company's founder, Louis Goldschmidt, established a fine-gauge knitting plant after spotting a trend towards lightweight clothing. Even today, Pantherella insists on using only the highest-quality yarns – cashmere, silk, and merino wool, for instance, as well as its bestselling line in Sea Island cotton. Pantherella has exclusive rights to make socks from genuine Sea Island cotton, so, unlike 'Sea Island quality', which is used by many of their competitors, this is the real deal – it's as strong as silk, as soft as cashmere and as long-lasting as wool; cool in summer, warm in winter.

Pantherella's other claim to fame is the socks' hand-linked toe seam, a skilled process that other sock manufacturers have rejected as too expensive. The process creates an invisible toe seam, which means increased comfort for the wearer. As for the correct sock etiquette, Savile Row tailors decree that no skin should be shown between the sock and trouser leg when sitting down.

BURLINGTON ARGYLE SOCKS
Where? www.sockshop.co.uk • All good department stores
How much? Approx £10/$15/€11
Burlington make the best brightly coloured argyle socks, which come complete with trademark stud. They're so good, in fact, that they even persuaded the 13th Duke of Argyle to star in one of their advertising campaigns – the diamond pattern is based on the Argyle tartan.

GAMMARELLI
Where? Via dei Cestari, Rome, Italy
How much? Approx £9/$13.50/€10
This shop is known as 'the Pope's couturier', as the boutique, which was established in 1798, has dressed virtually every Pope since then. It is best for bright cardinal-red socks, which are ribbed and come to the knee – some men have a fetish about such things. Also available in Archbishop Purple.

Stilettos

Manolo Blahnik

Where?

49–51 Old Church Street, London, SW3 • 00 44 207 352 8622 •
www.manoloblahnik.com

How much?

From £375/$734/€552

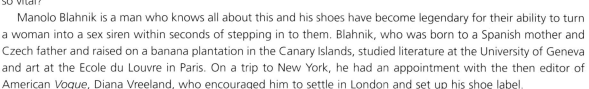

Madonna once described Manolo Blahnik's shoes as 'better than sex', adding 'what's more, they last longer'. She has a point. In an average lifetime, a woman spends up to three years of her life shopping, shelling out £31,680 on shoes. Is it any wonder, then, that the search for the perfect pair of stilettos is so vital?

Manolo Blahnik is a man who knows all about this and his shoes have become legendary for their ability to turn a woman into a sex siren within seconds of stepping in to them. Blahnik, who was born to a Spanish mother and Czech father and raised on a banana plantation in the Canary Islands, studied literature at the University of Geneva and art at the Ecole du Louvre in Paris. On a trip to New York, he had an appointment with the then editor of American *Vogue*, Diana Vreeland, who encouraged him to settle in London and set up his shoe label.

It is lucky for the women of the world that he did. From the outset of his career, Blahnik has had an instinct for proportion that has placed him above his competitors; his stilettos miraculously lengthen the leg from the hip

A QUICK Q&A WITH MANOLO BLAHNIK

Why does a stiletto heel change the way a woman looks so dramatically?

Manolo Blahnik: 'I adore the way a woman's body changes when she puts on heels; it is an instant transformation, no surgery necessary! From a technical point of view, when you raise the heel it forces the body to work completely differently.'

How does it alter her attitude?

MB: 'Shoes are always instant theatre, they help a person act who they want to be.'

When is a strap good? Any rules?

MB: 'Every single woman's legs are completely different and luckily there are endless options for straps. As a rule, an ankle strap will cut your leg, making it appear shorter, so if your legs are proportionately short, I would advise against straps. Each person must try everything on to find what works best for them.'

When should stilettos be worn?

MB: 'ALWAYS!'

When shouldn't stilettos be worn?

MB: 'If you are visiting an apartment or house with exquisite 18th-century parquet flooring.'

Your first memory of stilettos?

MB: 'Possibly my mother in shoes of her own design.'

Your favourite stiletto wearer of all time and why?

MB: 'All women in general!'

Christian Louboutin

right down to the tip of the toe and his classic shapes and styles are never overtly fashionable, remaining timelessly stylish. And while every celebrity from Nicole Kidman to Kylie Minogue has stepped out in a pair of Manolos, it is good old Marge Simpson, who wore a pair of his mules during a 1991 episode of *The Simpsons*, and, of course, *Sex and the City*'s Carrie Bradshaw, who symbolize exactly how culturally significant a pair of Manolo stilettos really are.

Christian Louboutin

CHRISTIAN LOUBOUTIN

Where? 23 Motcomb Street, London, SW1 • 00 44 207 245 6510 • www.christianlouboutin.com
How much? From approx £300/$450/€330
This French designer is known for his slim, vertiginous pencil-like heels with signature Chinese-red soles that have prompted men to follow women down the street upon seeing a flash of scarlet. Louboutin, who was inspired to become a shoe designer at the age of ten after spying a woman in an art gallery wearing the most striking pair of heels, says his shoes are 'a worktool or a weapon and an objet d'art'. As well as producing two collections of drop-dead sexy shoes a year, he works on private commissions – love letters and locks of hair are among the things that have been encased in those spiky, conical, wicked heels of his.

PIERRE HARDY

Where? Jardins du Palais-Royal, 156 Galerie de Valois, Paris, France • 00 33 1 42 605 975 • www.pierrehardy.com • Dover Street Market, 17-18 Dover Street, London, W1 • www.doverstreetmarket.com
How much? From about £400/$600/€445
After designing shoes for Hermès, Pierre Hardy launched his own collection in 1999. An instant hit, Hardy fast became identifiable for his super-sleek vertiginous heels, sculptural shapes and beautifully crafted uppers. In Paris, he is considered the king of the cobbling craft.

Pierre Hardy

Pierre Hardy

A SHORT HISTORY OF THE STILETTO

The inventive shoe designer, Salvatore Ferragamo, created the reinforced steel bar that gave rise to the stiletto heel in the 1950s. But it was French shoe designer Roger Vivier who took it one step further in the following decades, fully realizing the potential of the stiletto as an iconic heel shape. The stiletto heel is now one of the most stylish and important heel shapes in existence and features not only in exclusive designer shoe collections, but across the high street, too.

Sunglasses

Ray-Ban

Where?
www.raybansunglasses.co.uk •
Department stores
worldwide

How much?
Approx £105.95/
$155/€115

More than merely functional, sunglasses signify status, wealth and, above all else, image. One of the most iconic styles is the classic Ray-Ban Aviator. Army Air Corps commissioned Bausch & Lamb to design the teardrop-shaped Aviator in 1936 out of necessity – pilots had been suffering from headaches and nausea because of glare and the great distances they needed to travel. The name 'Ray-Ban' was chosen for the new product to emphasize the fact that the eyewear could 'ban' or block out the sun's rays and protect the wearer's eyes. In 1952, Ray-Ban launched a new model, the Wayfarer, a style that was promptly snapped up by Hollywood stars, including Audrey Hepburn, who wore a pair in *Breakfast at Tiffany's*. The Aviator was popularized again in the 1980s, when Tom Cruise wore them in *Top Gun*. Ray-Bans, recently enjoying a renaissance, remain timeless.

Ray-Ban

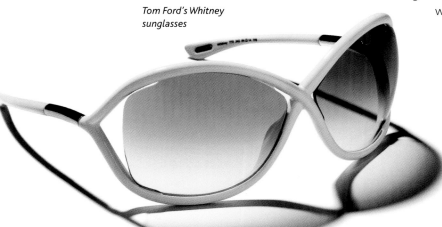

Tom Ford's Whitney sunglasses

TOM FORD
Where?
www.tomford.com •
Selfridges, 400 Oxford
Street, London, W1 •
0044 800 123 400
How much? From
£150/$225/€165
Not long after quitting as
Creative Director of Yves

Oliver Peoples' Harlot sunglasses

Saint Laurent, Tom Ford, the king of high-octane fashion, launched Tom Ford Eyewear. His sunglasses collection, with its streamlined, sleek and look-at-me styles, has gained instant credibility among the world's fashion fiends.

OLIVER PEOPLES

Where? www.oliverpeoples.com • Selected opticians worldwide

How much? Approx £245/$375/€275

A striking 70s-inspired style, Oliver Peoples' Harlot comes in a selection of shades, including bubble-gum pink, olive tortoiseshell and sophisticated mahogany brown. The LA brand, established in 1986, has fast become favoured by celebrities, including Kate Moss, who has made them famous by wearing the black version non-stop. Oliver Peoples has serious rock-and-roll credentials.

Say it with shades

- **Bottega Veneta:** For Milanese-style chic.
- **Chanel:** If only because of those tiny interlocking Cs on each side.
- **Dior:** Heir- and heiress-glamour; think Paris Hilton.
- **Roberto Cavalli:** The choice of the footballer and his wife for maximum show.
- **Yves Saint Laurent:** Refined with a dash of opulence.

WHICH STYLES SUIT WHICH FACE SHAPES BY TOP OPTOMETRIST, MICHEL GUILLON

- **Round** (soft, no angular features).
  Go for: contrast by adding feature: rectangular/hexagonal frames.

- **Square** (broad face with strong jaw and chin).
  Go for: rectangular elliptical frame with rounded softer corners.

- **Rectangular** (marked and more balanced features, as a square face, but not as wide).
  Go for: softer shape, oval to soften the image.

- **Triangular** (like a rectangular face but with narrow chin).
  Go for: small non-angular eye shape to minimize the difference in head width between the eye region and chin.

- **Oval** (soft regular features).
  Go for: the choice is yours, with any style you wish: discreet to minimize contrast, or bold to maximize impact.

Umbrella

Swaine Adeney Brigg

Where?
54 St James's Street, London, SW1 • 00 44 207
409 7277 • www.swaineadeney.co.uk

How much?
From approx £210/$315/€230

*Swaine
Adeney Brigg*

For the discerning gentleman, an umbrella is not just for keeping the rain off, but is a telling status symbol. Umbrellas may have been used in China and India for thousands of years before they ended up in England in the 18th century, but there's no doubt that the UK is now home to the best-quality umbrellas in the world. Swaine Adeney Brigg is as traditional a company as they come. Originating in 1836, it has been making umbrellas for the British royal family ever since. Its history is diverse, supplying luggage to Rolls Royce, Aston Martin and Bentley, as well as bullwhips for Indiana Jones in *Raiders of the Lost Ark*.

When it comes to umbrellas, the company's signature pieces include the Brigg Malacca umbrella handle, fashioned from Malaysian Mallaca cane, but the ultimate in luxury has to be the ebonized wood umbrella. There is also a ladies' parasol with a rhino horn handle, a snip at just £1,200. You wouldn't want to be leaving that on the train now, would you?

JAMES SMITH & SON
Where? 53 New Oxford St, London, WC1 • 00 44 207 836 4731 • www.james-smith.co.uk
How much? From approx £135/$205/€150
James Smith & Son has been a shrine to the umbrella since the 1850s. There is a bespoke service that allows you to choose the wood and colour you desire, as well as measuring the umbrella so that it is the right length when you walk. The elegant rosewood style is a fine-looking specimen.

*James
Smith &
Son*

PICKETT
Where? 32–33 Burlington Arcade, London, W1 • 00 44 207 493 8939 • www.pickett.co.uk
How much? From approx £69/$105/€76
This quality English leather accessories label offers a beautiful classic Malacca-handled umbrella. The epitome of understated British style.

Budget brollies

If the thought of spending upwards of £100 on an umbrella makes you giddy, go for a more practical foldaway option. A telltale sign of a good umbrella is the quality and quantity of rivets in the frame – make sure there are lots of them and that they are secure and well-made. One of the best foldaway umbrellas is the Knirp Duomatic Fiber T1. It features a carbonfibre frame and is rust-proof and, apparently, storm-proof. It is available at James Smith & Son (see above).

Wallet

Bottega Veneta

Where?
Stores worldwide including 33 Sloane Street, London, SW1 • 00 44 7 838 9394 • www.bottegaveneta.com

How much?
£267/$380/€288

Possibly the chicest Italian label in existence, Bottega Veneta's reputation was built on its unique woven leather accessories. A plain brown woven leather Bottega wallet from its classic 'The Knot' range spells style, class and refinement.

Bottega Veneta

COMME DES GARÇONS

Where? Dover Street Market, 17–18 Dover Street, London, W1 • 00 44 20 7518 0680 • www.doverstreetmarket.com

How much? From approx £109/$180/€126

This angular, leather wallet from the Japanese fashion label has become a must-have accessory among style mavens worldwide and a passport to cool. The trick is to find a variation on the style and colour that no-one else has seen. Look out for limited edition varieties.

DUNHILL

Where? 48 Jermyn Street, London, SW1 • 00 44 207 290 8600 • 711 Fifth Avenue, New York, NY • 001 212 753 9292 • www.dunhill.com

How much? From £150/$300/€220

This classic British brand, established by Alfred Dunhill in London's Mayfair in1907, is known for its luxury leather goods. Dunhill's classic wallets in either grained cowhide leather or mulsanne (a soft and supple leather with a natural finish) are quality classics that will last and last.

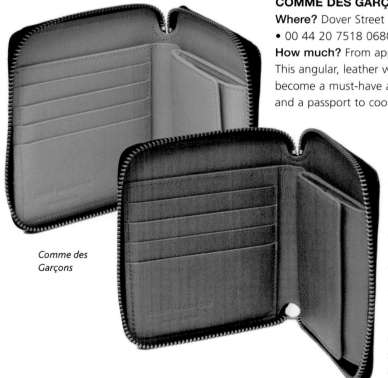

Comme des Garçons

Leisure

'They talk of the dignity of work.
The dignity is in leisure.'

Herman Melville,
American novelist and poet,
1819—1891

Bicycle

Pashley Princess Sovereign

Where?

Pashley Cycles, Masons Road, Stratford-upon-Avon, CV37 9NL • 00 44 1789 292 263 •
www.pashley.co.uk

How much?

Approx £533/$805/€590

First invented by Thomas Humber in 1868, bicycles are bound up in childhood memories: we all remember the first time the stabilizers came off and the joy of pedalling freely. Buying a bicycle is in many ways a more personal and sentimental process than buying a car or a scooter. And while there are thousands of high-tech, super-modern bikes in all sorts of shapes and sizes, none have the romance, history or aesthetic delights of William Pashley's elegant and traditional ladies' bicycles. Lovingly

Pashley Princess
Sovereign

handmade for over 70 years in Stratford-upon-Avon, this quintessentially English bicycle features a front basket, five-speed alloy hub gears and a Brooks leather saddle with springs that mould to your bottom. The Princess Sovereign, available in Regency Green, Buckingham Black, or Rich Burgundy, is stylish, classic and a pleasure to ride. The brand was recently propelled to the big screen: Cate Blanchett rode one most elegantly in *Notes on a Scandal*.

SCHWINN CRUISERS

Where? www.schwinnbike.com

How much? From approx £197/$299/€220

Founded in the United States in 1895, Schwinn was one of the original purveyors of the modern bicycle. The company has since brought us many classic bikes, including the stylized Sting-Ray – with its high-rise handlebars, 'banana' seat and enlarged back wheel – in 1963, and the BMX in 1970. Its fabulously lightweight Whitewall Typhoon cruiser tyre is the original smooth roller for easy riding, featuring corrosion-resistant alloy wheels and stainless-steel spokes. The Cruiser has classic, curvy, 1950s' styling and a two-tone colourway.

SÖGRENI OF COPENHAGEN

Where? Sankt Peder Straede 30A, 1453 Copenhagen, Denmark • 00 45 33 127 879 • www.sogreni.dk

How much? From approx £9,885/$14,965/€11,000

Started by Soren Sögreni in 1981, this Copenhagen showroom caters for the city's prolific cycling population with its beautifully simple bicycles made from quality materials – each model has an equal measure of technical brilliance and subtle good looks. The 'Sögreni Classic', available in both men's and women's versions, is the quintessential modern bicycle.

Cigar

Partagas Reserva Serie D No 4.

Where?

Direct from the facory in Havana: Calle Industria 520, between Dragones and Barcelona, Centro Habana • Davidoff, 35 St James's Street, London, SW1 • 00 44 207 930 3079 • www.davidoff.com • Hunters & Frankau • 00 44 207 471 8400 • www.cigars.co.uk

How much?

A box of 20 costs £548/$1,054/€800

The best cigars are hand-rolled Cuban numbers, known in the trade as 'Havanas'. Cuban cigars are so good because the country's soil and climate is ideal for growing tobacco, and, rather like a fine wine, age brings out their flavour. Havana houses a number of world-renowned cigar manufacturers, including Cohiba, Montecristo and Partagas, one of the oldest, which makes cigars in much the same way it did when the factory opened in the 1840s.

One thing that *has* changed, though, is the 'reserva'. Launched early in 2005, reserva is predicted to add a new layer of luxury to the world of handmade cigars. Reserva refers to specially selected tobacco leaves that have been fermented for longer – as long as five years, in fact; a single year is much more usual. So already they're more flavoursome than most. Add to that the fact that the binder, the substance that holds together the filler made up of leaves, and the wrapper have also been aged for five years and, well, you have something rather special.

The best brands – Montecristo, Cohiba, Partagas – have all got their hands on reserva cigars, each limited to 5,000 numbered boxes. Partagas' Reserva 'torpedo' cigars, which are tapered at the end, have been introduced as part of Serie D, already a renowned line. Not only do these cigars taste fantastic, they also make a wise investment. Christie's holds twice-yearly cigar auctions – those from before the 1963 Cuban embargo are especially coveted – so if connoisseurs are going mad for the Partagas Reserva now, imagine what they'll be doing in 20 years time. Investment cigars should be stored correctly; many suppliers offer storage facilities.

COHIBA DOUBLE CORONA

Where? J.J. Fox & Robert Lewis, 19 St James's Street, London, SW1 • 00 44 207 930 3787 • www.jjfox.co.uk

How much? Approx £65/$98/€72 per cigar

This is the most expensive cigar offered by esteemed cigar sellers Fox's. Impossibly smooth and sophisticated, many aficionados claim this is the best cigar they have ever smoked.

VINTAGE DUNHILLS AND DAVIDOFFS

Where? www.cgarsltd.co.uk

How much? For one Davidoff Chateau Y'Quem cigar: £200/$300/€222

Dunhills and Davidoffs made before 1992 – in other words, when they were still being made in Cuba – are particularly prized. The ultimate? Davidoff Chateau Y'Quem. In the cigar world, incidentally, anything pre-1995 is vintage.

Partagas Reserva Serie D No 4.

Camera

Leica MP

Leica MP

Where?
www.leica-camera.com •
Various outlets worldwide
How much?
£2,975 for the camera and
£1,819 for lense

The digital age is upon us, with pundits predicting that film will soon be a thing of the past. Leica aficionados beg to differ, believing that these are the only cameras worth hanging round your neck, thanks to an unusually quiet shutter release, a commanding ability to take excellent pictures in even the gloomiest of light and, of course, handsome good looks. With a Leica you must wind the film on yourself and learn how to use a rangefinder – a separate viewfinder and focusing device. All these niggling idiosyncrasies are part of the reason why Leicas are so well-loved.

> '*The Leica has timeless styling, a classic form and always produces the very highest quality images.*'
> **Sir Paul Smith, British designer and keen photographer**

The German company has been making cameras since 1925 and actually invented 35-mm photography. Leicas entered photography mythology when Henri Cartier-Bresson, who was never seen without his Leica, buried his in the ground when he thought he was going to be captured during the Second World War.

The MP was first launched in 1956, and models from the 1950s and 1960s are now highly collectable. It was cleverly relaunched in 2003, and the company went on to sell more cameras than it had since 1968. The MP model is still made by hand and, of course, includes a Leica lens – said to be the best. There is even an 'à la carte' service that allows Leica lovers to custom-build their camera; choices include Hermès calfskin. The Leica is even easy to repair; indeed, the company guarantees that new owners will be able to get hold of parts for their camera for at least 30 years after purchasing, something refreshing in a disposable consumer culture such as ours. No wonder people like Leica a lot.

CONTAX T2

Where? From second-hand camera dealers, or try online sellers such as eBay
How much? The price varies, but expect to pay around £200/$300/€222
This discontinued camera is still the off-duty choice of many a fashion photographer – Mario Testino claims he carries one at all times. In fact, in recent years the Contax T2 has been used increasingly in professional shoots, with Terry Richardson and Juergen Teller (he uses one for those iconic Marc Jacobs ads) among its fans. Professionals love the 'verité' this point-and-shoot can produce. A cult choice.

CANON'S IXUS RANGE

Where? Good electrical suppliers • www.canon.co.uk
How much? From approx £200/$300/€222
A pocket-sized digital camera that is also stylish and gives fantastic results; no wonder the Ixus line is so popular. Available in a range of colours, its USPs include a large LCD screen, image stabilizer, and red-eye reduction.

Classic car

Aston Martin DB5

Where?

www.astonmartin.com •

www.autotraderclassics.com •

Classic car dealers

How much?

Price varies according to dealer

Aston Martin DB5

Cars have become one of the most pioneering and designed objects of the modern age, and are now among the most state-of-the-art, technologically exciting purchases you can make. But nothing carries quite the same cachet as a classic car. A symbol of style, class and refinement, a beautifully designed old-fashioned motor will garner raised eyebrows from across the street and – quite literally – stop traffic.

If there is one classic car that reigns high above the rest in terms of cool and good looks, it is a Bond car. The sleek and curvaceous Aston Martin DB5 is the one Sean Connery famously drove in *Goldfinger* – although his was equipped with machine guns, bulletproof shields, ejector seat and revolving licence plates. Founded in the UK by Lionel Martin and Robert Bamford in 1914, Aston Martin soon made a name for itself by making zippy racing cars, producing several for the French Grand Prix in the 1920s. In 1947, the company was bought by Sir David Brown – who gave his initials to the series to which the DB5 belongs. Only 886 of these cars were ever built, so you'll have to look long and hard if you want one, although you could, of course, opt for another model in the DB range. To this day, an exceptional level of workmanship goes into each Aston Martin produced. A classic, stylish choice.

JAGUAR E-TYPE

Where? www.jaguar.com • Classic car dealers • Henry Pearman of Eagle E-Types • 00 44 1825 830 966 • ww.eaglegb.com

How much? From around £10,000 for an average 2+2 Series 2 to £75,000 for an E-Type Roadster in good nick

Also known as the E-type or XK-E, this magnificent car was designed by Malcolm Sayer, an aerodynamics engineer, and is distinctive due to its elongated bonnet and sleek, aeroplane-like structure. The fact that it could reach 150mph (241km/h) and cost half the price of its competitors when it was launched in 1963 caused a sensation. Sayer claimed it was the first car to be 'mathematically designed'. It was also the first sports car to be mass-produced – over 70,000 were built, which means it should be possible to track down a second-hand model within a few months. Then again, you can always opt for Jaguar's new take on the E-type, complete with a sleek, leather interior, control console with switches and baritone exhaust.

VOLVO P1800

Where? www.volvoclub.org.uk • volvo1800pictures.com • www.practicalclassics.co.uk

How much? From about £3,000/$4,540/€3,338

Yes it's a Volvo, the Swedish car manufacturers known for their angular and practical cars, but the P1800 also happens to be the company's coolest model. It shot to fame in the 1960s after appearing as Roger Moore's preferred mode of transport in *The Saint*, and possesses a robust engine, an aerodynamic look and stylized fins. Less showy than a Bentley or Merc – a hip and affordable option.

Golf driver

TaylorMade R7

Where?
www.taylormadegolf.com • www.golfbuyitonline.co.uk
How much?
Approximately £289/$440/€320

> **'G**olf is a game that is played on a five-inch course – the distance between your ears.'
>
> **Bobby Jones, championship golfer**

TaylorMade R7

A driver has been described as 'the club that separate contenders from the pretenders'. It is also the most expensive club in the bag, something that should also include a variety of woods, irons, a pitching wedge and a putter – golf rules allow a maximum of 14 clubs.

A driver is what a golfer uses to whack the ball when he or she tees-off – 'drive for show, putt for dough', so the saying goes – and male players, in particular, are obsessed with the length of their tee. The TaylorMade R7 is truly revolutionary. A driver that's currently most popular with professionals, as well as amateurs who can afford it, it is so prized, in fact, that many professional players use this brand for no financial reward.

The TaylorMade brand is renowned for its innovative use of new technology, and the R7 is no different, made up of a series of weights that can be adjusted using a special wrench to six different 'launch settings'. It is illegal to walk around a course adjusting the head of your clubs; instead, you set the driver to work around your weaknesses. When the R7 was first introduced a couple of years ago, it astounded the golf world. TaylorMade has since conceded that the R7 has a 95 percent satisfaction rating and quite rightly describe it as 'the most highly awarded driver in the world'.

The company was started in Illinois in 1979 after the founder, Gary Adams, discovered balls struck by metal drivers travelled much further than those struck by traditional woods. Other brands worth buying for your bag include Titleist and Ping.

CALLAWAY FTIQ
Where? www.callawaygolf.com • www.golferseagle.com
How much? From £299/$450/€330
The number-one selling brand in the United States (TaylorMade is number two), this driver is a mix of titanium and carbon, excellent for power and precision.

CLEVELAND LAUNCHER
Where? www.clevelandgolf.com
How much? From £299/$450/€330
A model with a big titanium head, this is the perfect driver for those with a high handicap.

Scooter

Vespa GTS250

Where?
www.vespa.com
How much?
Approx £3,475/$3,250/€3,866

Vespa GTS250

Vepsa is Italian for 'wasp' – and if you've ever heard one of these scooters zipping down a street, you'll know why. The vehicle was invented by Rinaldo Piaggio as the perfect cheap vehicle to get Italy moving again in the postwar period. He instructed his designers to create a scooter that was suitable for both men and women, could take a passenger and wouldn't get clothes dirty – crucial for fashion-conscious Italians.

The first Vespa was introduced in Italy in 1946 and was an immediate success, since it proved skilful at dodging the country's bomb-scarred roads. Since then, Vespa has sold more than 16 million scooters worldwide and notable models include the LX, made famous by Audrey Hepburn in the film *Roman Holiday*, and the ET2, which arrived on the scene in 1996 and helped invigorate sales in urban areas (this is the model Gwyneth Paltrow rides).

The GTS250 is the latest and most powerful Vespa yet and is an updated version of the GS (the Grand Sport), a model that is on permanent display at the Museum of Modern Art in New York. The GTS250 has Vespa's trademark rounded body and a top speed of 76mph (122 km/h) – it is so fast, in fact, that you'll need a motorcycle licence to ride it in the UK. Design features include a bar-mounted headlight and fold-down chrome rear rack headlight, plenty of underseat storage and a glove compartment.

Scooters have had a renaissance over the last few years, as commuters realize that they offer the quickest way of getting around increasingly congested cities. The updated features of the Vespa make it appealing to both sexes – men love the chrome-ringed instrument panel that looks like it belongs to an Italian sports car, while women wax lyrical about the 'curry rack' which is designed for hanging takeaways – or handbags.

PIAGGIO ZIP
Where? www.piaggio-scooters.co.uk
How much? From £1,077/$1,630/€1,190
A ubiquitous sight on London's roads, this is the perfect urban model – cheap and easy to get around.

LAMBRETTA LD150
Where? Various specialist vintage dealers, including www.supersonicscooters.com and www.lambretta.co.uk
How much? Around £1,750/$2,650/€1,950
Lambretta was the main competition for Vepsa in the 1950s and 1960s. This model has two separate seats and is capable of 52mph (84km/h). It is still popular, although production ceased in the 1970s.

Skis

 K2

Where?
www.k2skis.com •
Snow and Rock • www.snowandrock.com
How much?
From £250/$370/€280

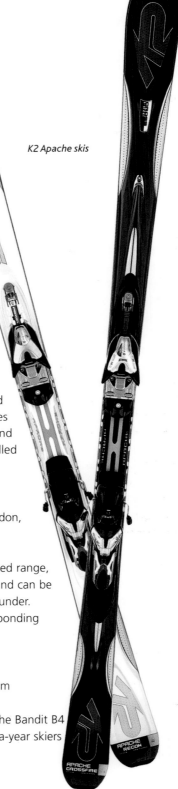

K2 Apache skis

Rock paintings depict hunters skiing over 5,000 years ago and the Swedish army trained on skis in the 18th century, but the first skis resembling those we know today were invented in Norway in the 19th century. In 1928, the first aluminium ski was produced in France. Today, skis are shorter, wider and curvier than ever, with a greater variety of styles for varying levels of skill, though it's important you pick skis to suit your needs whether you're off for a week of on-piste skiing or a season of extreme off-piste endeavour. When it comes to skis, size and shape count. While jackets, salopettes and glasses are all of vital importance, the true skier knows that a good-quality pair of skis is paramount. It's not about simply buying the most expensive pair, but the ones that best suit your requirements. K2 is a fine Canadian brand that has devised skis for the expert skier. The Apache range provides particularly impressive specimens that can be used in any conditions and on any terrain, due to their expert construction from a material called Titan Metal Laminate.

VOLKL

Where? www.voelkl.com • Ellis Brigham, 3–11 Southampton Street, London, WC2 • 00 44 207 395 1010 • www.ellisbrigham.com
How much? From £283/$392/€307
This German brand offers a wide selection of skis, including the Unlimited range, which combines optimum ski width with the right amount of side cut and can be adapted to every ski style and level. In other words, this is a great all-rounder. Volkl's skis are also equipped with 'Double Grip' LT design and a corresponding absorption system.

ROSSIGNOL

Where? www.rossignol.com • Snow and Rock • www.snowandrock.com
How much? From £335/$500/€370
An excellent brand with a wide range of skis, particularly for women. The Bandit B4 is good for free-riding, while the Open is excellent for those one-week-a-year skiers who want control and carving power.

Tennis racquet

Babolat Pure Storm

Where?
www.babolat.com • www.racket-sport.com •
www.tennis-warehouse.com
Good sports shops worldwide

How much?
From £101/$185/€112

Tennis dates back to the Tudor period, but the racquet has progressed greatly since then. Back in 1900, lawn tennis was big and racquets were small and loosely strung with grooved handles. In the 1920s, frames were made from solid ash and strung with piano wire. By the 1950s, metal was also being used to make frames, and by the 1980s, graphite racquets reigned supreme. Today, tennis racquets are generally lighter, with larger heads that improve control and speed. But what's the best of them all? While technology is constantly moving forward, Babolat's Pure Drive is currently considered one of the best racquets you can buy. Babolat has over 125 years experience at making top-notch designs. The 'Woofer' system generates power, since inside the frame are four symmetrical pulleys that contract on contact. The ball stays on the strings a split second longer – or so it feels – then bounces off with extra force. That is probably why Andy Roddick uses this brand for his record-breaking 155mph (250km/h) serve.

Babolat Pure Storm

WILSON NCODE NTOUR

Where? www.bellracquetsports.com • www.wilson.com
How much? £114/$223/€168

This lightweight frame is used by Lindsay Davenport. Gaps in the graphite frame are filled with silicone, which results in less vibration, more control and is less likely to cause tennis elbow. Wilson also claim this racquet is twice as strong and stable as a normal racquet and up to 22 percent more powerful than an ordinary graphite frame. The head is larger than usual and good for intermediate players who still want some pop from the racquet, while gaining control. For keen amateurs, Wilson is also the chicest choice.

PRINCE O3 SILVER

Where? www.princetennis.com • www.racket-sport.com
How much? £160/$260/€234

Large 'O' ports around the frame give this racquet extra spring, which means it moves through the air more quickly, making it easier to return those smashes. Those 'O's also create a bigger sweet spot (the area on the strings that produces the best combination of feel and power), so it takes minimal energy to hit the ball and the player is able to focus on technique.